CW01668294

Images of Aran

PHOTOGRAPHS BY FATHER BROWNE

1925 & 1938

A summary of Father Browne's remarkable life is given in the Introduction. A hero of World War I, decorated many times for bravery, Father Browne was a keen photographer who took over 42,000 pictures in over thirty countries between 1897 and 1957 — including his famous *Titanic* photographs. These Aran images were taken on his first visit to the islands in 1925 and during his lengthy stay in 1938.

The full story of Father Frank Browne S.J. is told in the biography, *A Life in Pictures* (Wolfhound Press, 1994). His biographer, E. E. O'Donnell S.J. holds a Ph.D. in Communication from the University of Southern California at Los Angeles. As curator of the Father Browne S.J. Collection — and its re-discoverer in 1985 — he has been responsible for bringing the photographs to public attention through books, television documentaries and exhibitions that have been held all over Ireland and England and at the Centre Georges Pompidou, Paris.

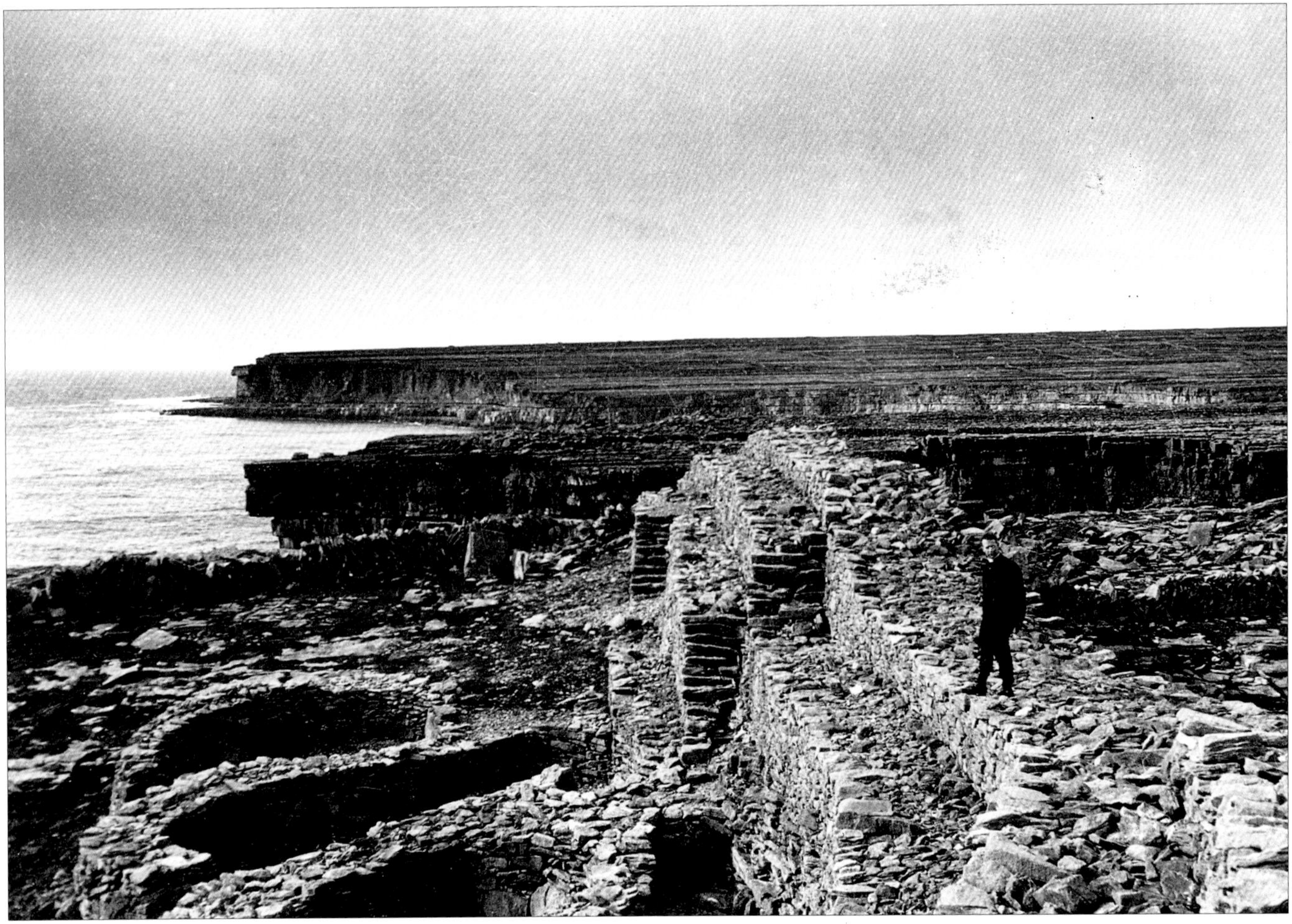

Father Frank Browne S.J. photographed on the ramparts
of Dún Dúchathair by his colleague, Father John Keane S.J., in 1925.

Images of Aran

PHOTOGRAPHS BY FATHER BROWNE

1925 & 1938

E.E. O'Donnell S.J.

WOLFHOUND PRESS

and in the US & Canada

The Irish American Book Company

First published 1998 by
WOLFHOUND PRESS Ltd
68 Mountjoy Square
Dublin 1
Tel: (+353-1) 8740354
Fax: (+353-1) 8720207

Distributed in the US & Canada by
The Irish American Book Company (IABC)
6309 Monarch Park Place
Suite 101
Niwot, Colorado 80503, USA
Tel: (+303) 652 2710/Fax: (+303) 652 2689

British Library Cataloguing in Publication Data
A catalogue record for this book is available from the British Library

ISBN 0-86327-599-0

Cover design: Slick Fish Design, Dublin
Typesetting & layout: Wolfhound Press
Duotone reproduction and film: Reprolink, Dublin
Photographic prints: Davison & Associates, Dublin
Printed and bound in Spain by Estudios Gráficos Zure

Profits made by the Jesuit Order from the sale of Father Browne's books and prints go to the Jesuit Solidarity Fund established to help counteract Ireland's serious unemployment problems both north and south of the border.

Photographic prints are available from Davison & Associates, 69B Heather Road, Sandyford Industrial Estate, Dublin 18, Ireland.

ALSO BY E. E. O'DONNELL S.J.

Published by Wolfhound Press
The Annals of Dublin (1987)
Father Browne's Ireland (1988)
The Genius of Father Browne (1989)
Father Browne's Dublin (1990)
Father Browne: A Life in Pictures (1991)
Father Browne's Cork (1992)
Father Browne's Australia (1995)
Father Browne's England (1996)
Father Browne's Titanic *Album: A Passenger's Photographs & Personal Memoir (1997)*
This book also published in the USA as *The Last Days of the Titanic]*

Published by The Society of Irish Foresters
Forest Images: Father Browne's Woodland Photographs (1993)

Published by Anatolia Editions, Paris
L'Irlande du Père Browne (1996)
[This title is available directly from the author]

CONTENTS

Introduction

The reputation of Father Frank Browne S.J. as a photographer has grown constantly since the rediscovery of his 42,000 negatives in 1985. The books of his pictures, a six-part television series and numerous exhibitions in Ireland, France and Germany have made his name better known with each year that passes. Books featuring his English and Australian photographs have been widely appreciated in those two countries.

Although a major exhibition of his work was shown in 1996 at the Pompidou Centre in Paris — where it was seen by 40,000 people a day for six weeks — Father Browne's name is still unfamiliar to the average citizen of mainland Europe. And he has yet to be introduced to Japan and to the United States of America. Since many American, Japanese and European visitors come to visit Aran each year, I think a short introduction to the photographer would be in order here.

Francis Mary Hegarty Browne was born in Cork in 1880. The youngest of eight children, he came from a distinguished family, his grandfather being Lord Mayor of Cork and his uncle, Robert Browne, the bishop of the neighbouring diocese of Cloyne for nearly forty years.

Educated at the Bower Convent, Athlone, and at Belvedere and Castleknock Colleges in Dublin, Frank took his first photographs a century ago when he toured Europe before joining the Jesuits in 1897. After a two-year noviceship near Tullamore, Frank moved to Dublin where he attended the Royal University for three years as a strict contemporary of James Joyce. "Mr Browne the Jesuit" features several times in *Finnegans Wake.*

From 1902 to 1905 Frank Browne studied philosophy in the north of Italy. Then he returned to Dublin to teach for six years at Belvedere College. In 1911 he began his theological studies at Milltown Park, Dublin, where he was ordained a priest in 1915. It was during this time, in April 1912 to be precise, that his Uncle Robert sent him a first-class ticket for the maiden voyage of the *Titanic* from Southampton to Queenstown. His account of that voyage — and the pictures he took on board the doomed liner — were published by Wolfhound Press in 1997.

After his ordination, Father Browne was appointed chaplain to the Irish Guards and headed for Flanders. For the duration of World War I he served in the front lines where he was injured five times and gassed once. His commanding officer, Colonel (later Field Marshal Earl of Tunis) Alexander described him as "the bravest man I ever met." Indeed Father Browne became one of the most decorated chaplains of the war, winning the British Military Cross and Bar and the French *Croix de Guerre* and he was also personally honoured by King Albert of Belgium.

During 1919 the chaplain served with the Irish Guards in Germany. The album of photographs which he took in Cologne, Bonn and Koblenz, entitled "The Watch on the Rhine", is still extant.

In 1920 he returned to Dublin where he soon became Superior of St Francis Xavier's Church, Gardiner Street. Due to the mustard gas he had inhaled near Ypres during the war, his lungs began to deteriorate and he was sent to the warmer climate of Australia for two years. This cure worked well and when he returned to Dublin in 1925 he was able to resume his office.

In 1927 Father Browne was instrumental in mounting Ireland's first International Salon of Photography. As the years went by, he became more and more adept behind the camera, his prize-winning medals turning from bronze to gold. In 1929 he became a member of the Jesuit Retreats & Missions Staff, an appointment he held for the rest of his life. This work brought him to nearly every parish in Ireland as well as to many places in England, Wales and Scotland.

In England Father Browne was commissioned to take photographs for the British Museum and for the Church of England. In return for the articles he contributed to *The Kodak Magazine* in the 1930s, he was given free film for life.

At the outbreak of World War II in 1939, Father Browne volunteered to serve as chaplain to the Irish Guards once again. His Superior informed him rather curtly that the Republic of Ireland was neutral in this conflict whereas in 1914-18 Ireland had been part of the United Kingdom.

The priest's pastoral activities were confined to Ireland until 1945, which helps to explain why 36,000 of his photographs were taken in this country. Father Browne was based at Emo in County Laois until 1957 when he was transferred to Dublin, where he died three years later. Lord Nugent wrote his obituary in *The Irish Guards Association Journal,* where he said:

> Everyone in the Battalion, officer or man, Catholic or Protestant, loved and respected Father Browne and he had great influence for good. He was a brave man in the true sense for he was conscious of danger but never allowed shells or bullets, which he hated as much as any of us, to divert him from his duty. Where the wounded or dying lay, there Father Browne was to be found to give them comfort and peace ... A great Christian, a brave and lovable man, we who knew him so well will always be grateful for his friendship and for the example that he set.

For twenty-five years after his death Father Browne's meticulously captioned negatives lay buried in the Jesuit archives in Dublin. I happened to find them in 1985 and was soon told that my treasure trove might disappear again. The negatives were on a nitrate-based material that was disintegrating. To save the collection, it would be necessary to transfer the images to safety-film — a job that would cost many thousands of pounds. Fortunately, Allied Irish Bank came to the rescue and had the negatives restored. Since then, the bank's subsidiary company, Ark Life, has been showing exhibitions of the photographs all over Ireland.

The Guinness Hopstore held a major exhibition of the Dublin photographs and Radio Telefís Éireann, Ireland's national television corporation, has aired a six-part series, *The Day before Yesterday,* twice. A French book, *L'Irlande du père Browne* was published by Anatolia Editions, Paris, and *Father Browne's Woodland Photographs* was published by the Society of Irish Foresters. A further eight books, including my biography of the photographer, are published by Wolfhound Press.

The photographs in this book were taken in 1925 and 1938. On his first visit to the Aran Islands, Father Browne's time was limited and we get the impression that he was only there for a matter of days. He had just returned from his two-year stay in Australia so, presumably, he did not want to absent himself for much longer from his job as Superior of Gardiner Street Church in Dublin.

In 1938 his time on the islands was much longer. It lasted for at least three weeks and he took nearly 750 photographs on all three islands during this time. Father Browne was very interested in history and prehistory. In his own index to the collection he has a section entitled 'Prehistoric Ireland' where he lists the pictures he took of cromlechs or dolmens, megalithic tombs, inscribed stones and so forth. Newgrange, before it was restored, is an interesting example in his category. On Aran, therefore, he was more than a little keen on seeing and recording the prehistoric forts. He photographed every one of them, inside and out.

Father Browne left very few 'positive' photographs behind him. To be exact, he left ten albums with about a hundred pictures in each. In order words, he himself saw only 1,000 of his 42,000 photographs as positives. Two of the ten albums were entitled 'The Monasteries of Ireland' and included photos from nearly all of the country's thirty-two counties. This goes to show how fascinated he was by the religious ruins of ancient Ireland. When he visited Aran in 1938, therefore, he took care to photograph all the ecclesiastical ruins, the crosses and pieces of crosses, the holy wells and pilgrimage sites.

Because he conducted pilgrimages himself, Father Browne was specially interested in photographing the Aran sites where these took place - for example, the monastic site at na Seacht dTeampaill. These would later be indexed in his files of negatives with places like Lough Derg, Glencolmcille and Croagh Patrick in Ireland, with Walsingham and Dunwich in England and with pilgrims' paths on the islands of Scotland and Jura in Scotland.

Wherever Father Browne went, he loved to photograph the local people: men, women and children. Examples of his technique can be seen in this book where we are given good illustrations of what the island people looked like in the 1920s and 1930s.

Happily Browne was in Oughill on the day of a wedding. He was often invited to photograph weddings but he rarely had the chance to record one like this. Where else would you see the bridesmaid smoking a cigarette?

Finally, a word or two about the logic of this book, where each chapter has its own introductory preamble. I begin with the prehistoric remains both to give a sense of chronology and because these are what many people go to Aran to see. Next there is a chapter on currachs and other boats, the former being the kind of vessel that the prehistoric fort-builders arrived in. From these we move into the historic period of ancient Celtic Christianity. These ecclesiastical buildings were constructed over a span of one thousand years, from the fifth to the fifteenth century. Because the islanders still refer to their home as 'Ara na Naomh', Aran of the Saints, this chapter is longer than the others.

After that I give a chapter on the main occupations of the islanders. These have changed a lot since the introduction of electricity long after Father Browne's 1938 visit. This is followed by a short chapter on the land and the sea, placed here both by way of interlude — to separate the photographs of people — and because the barren rock and the often wild Atlantic play such a central part in the lives of the islanders. Since Father Browne's last visit, the introduction of the air service has made a crucial psychological difference in the mentality of the people of Aran. Because the aeroplanes fly even when the boats are unable to sail, the people no longer feel so isolated. They no longer have to worry about somebody in need of hospitalisation being unable to reach the mainland.

Then comes the chapter on the islanders themselves and I am very grateful to them for helping me to identify every person that Father Browne photographed so long ago. I do not believe that the like could happen anywhere else in Ireland.

Still connected with the people of Aran, I conclude with two chapters of local historic interest: a wedding and a lifeboat rescue. The photographer was lucky to be on Aran in August of that year when these two happy events took place.

In 1938 the annual number of visitors to Aran was 300. Today the figure is over 15,000. Both in 1925 and in 1938 Father Browne, like most visitors, travelled on the *Dun Aengus*, a ship that served the islanders faithfully for forty-six years. That is why I begin with a shot of the steamer arriving at Kilronan and conclude with the final picture the photographer took as he left Aran for the last time.

[Note: the photographs all date from 1938 unless otherwise indicated in captions]

Captain Meskell brings the SS *Dun Aengus* alongside the pier at Kilronan. Beside him stands the mate, Michael Folan. Most of the passengers are tourists. Among the islanders on board are Margaret Dirrane and Winnie Faherty.

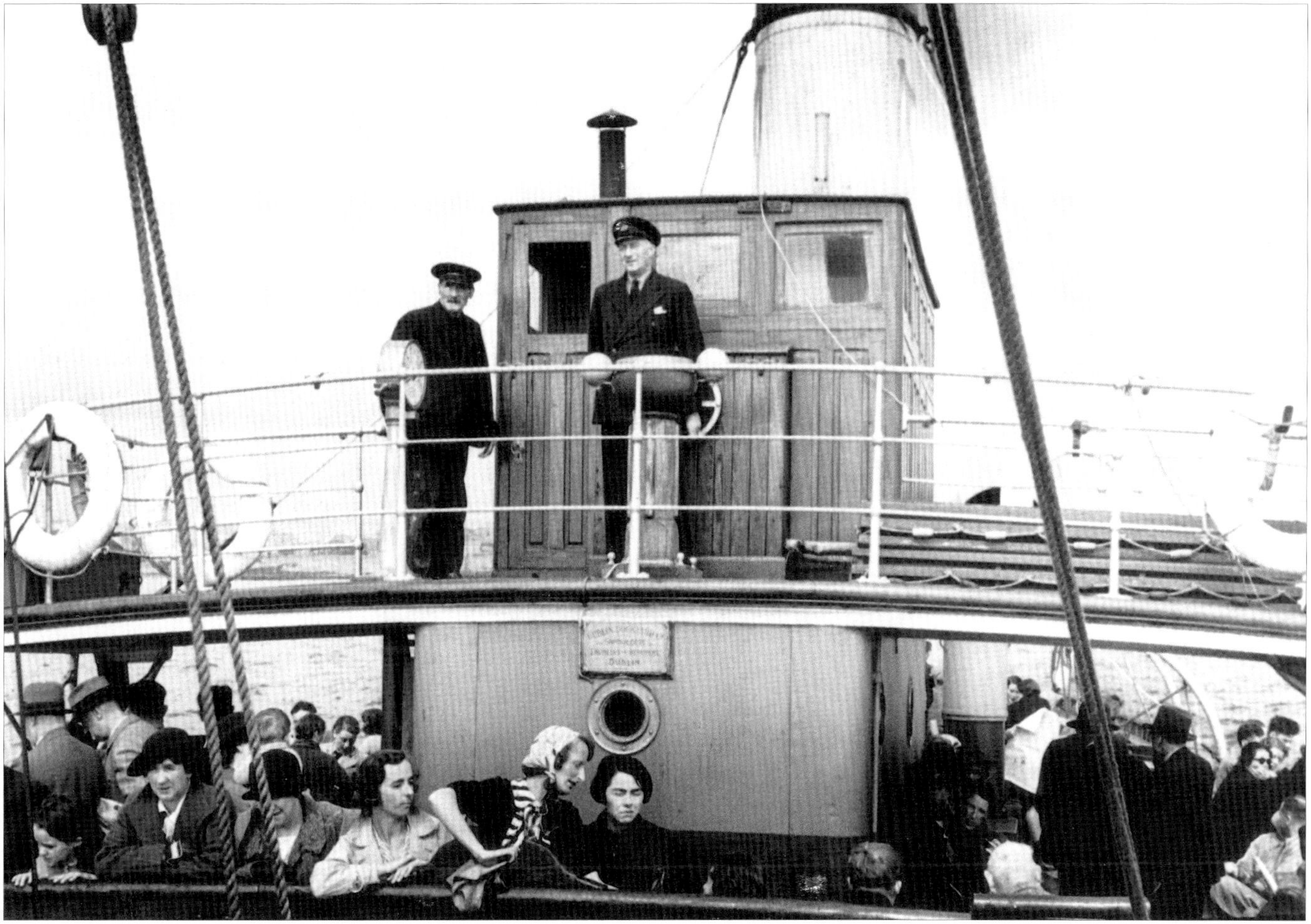

Spelling

The names of people in this book are spelt in the way they were given either to Father Browne or to myself during my research trips to Aran. That explains, for example, why a common surname is sometimes given as Conneely, sometimes as Ó Congaile.

The names of saints are given in their most modern form, whether in Irish or English. St Enda, for instance, is normally written Naomh Éinne, even though the ship plying between Galway and the islands for many years was the *Naomh Éanna.*

Since this book is likely to be read by more visitors than natives of Aran, I have given place-names in English where these are commonly anglicised. Thus I use Kilronan, Kilmurvey, Onaght etc in the same way as I would write Rome, Munich or Lisbon, even though the natives of these places spell them in their own language. Whenever I thought it helpful, I have given names in both languages.

As regards the spellings of the islands themselves, since both Irish and English are in common usage and sound roughly the same, I have settled for the Irish spellings, Inis Mór, Inis Meáin and Inis Oírr. It should not take the foreigner long to learn these words for Inishmore, Inishmaan and Inisheer.

Finally, there is the spelling of 'Aran' itself. I have used this spelling throughout because the Irish, Árainn, is used ambiguously in recent books, sometimes referring to Inis Mór and at other times referring to all three islands. For me, Aran is the name of the group. Note that there is no such name as 'The Arans' just as there is no such place as 'The Orkneys' - despite this usage by the BBC and some quality English newspapers.

The doorway into the inner citadel at Dún Aonghasa. The dimensions of the door show that cattle as well as people could have come here for sanctuary during times of invasion.

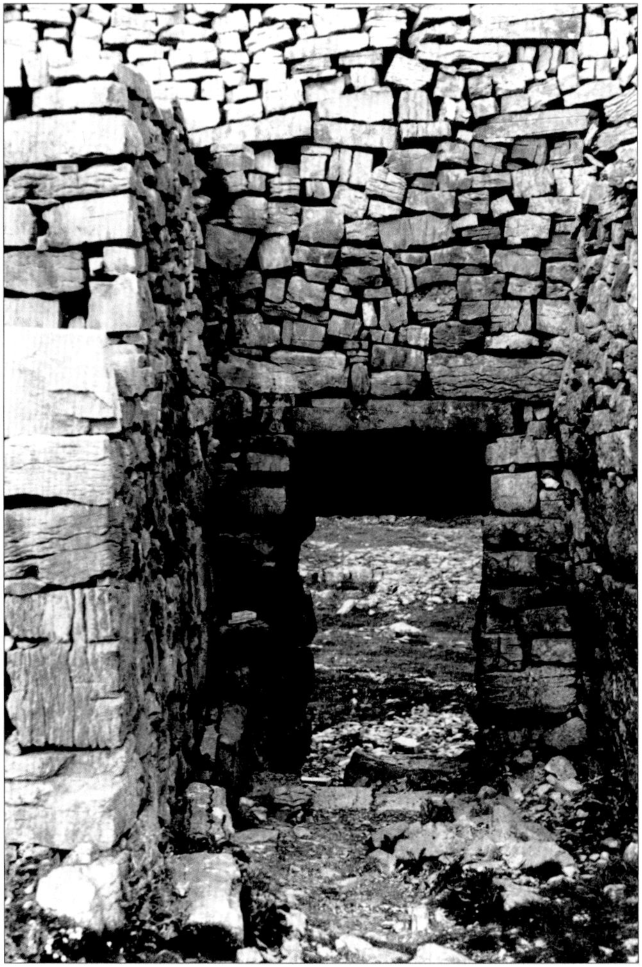

Chapter I

Prehistoric Aran

From all I have read about the archaeology of Aran, it seems to me that, to date, the experts have come up with more questions than answers. Whenever archaeologists do provide an answer, it appears to be contradicted by the majority of their *confrères*. There is disagreement about practically all of the prehistoric buildings on Aran, both civil and military, and its main source seems to be conflicting ideas as to who built them.

Until recently there seemed to be some broad agreement that the great Stone Age tombs and forts of Ireland were first built in the eastern half of the country and then gradually moved westwards. Nowadays, the revisionist and widely accepted view is actually the very reverse. Our great national monuments of the megalithic period were first built in the western half of the country and moved, it now appears, from Sligo in the west (e.g. Carrowmore) through the Midlands (e.g. Loughcrew) to the Boyne Valley of the east (e.g. Newgrange). This view is based on the assumption that the builders sailed here from mainland Europe and made landfalls in places likes the Dingle Peninsula and the Aran Islands. In Dingle they left stone forts and *clocháns*, or stone houses, at places like Ballynavenooragh. On Aran they left the stone forts and *clocháns* that are the subject of this chapter.

Dún Aonghasa (Dun Aengus) is the best known and most studied of the Aran forts but even here we have disagreement about its date and purpose. Literary legend tells us that it was built by Aonghas, a chief of the Fir Bolg (Belgic Celts?) back in the mists of time, i.e. at least 1000 B.C. Modern scholars disagree, some saying it could have been built as recently as 1000 A.D. by a Scot called Angus, others dating it to approximately 100 B.C. All we know for sure is that it stands on the edge of a 275-feet-high cliff and that, towards the end of the last century, it was considerably altered by conservationists who built the huge buttresses which support the walls today.

Some experts maintain that we now have only half a fort, the other half having collapsed into the Atlantic. Personally I find this hard to credit since such an enormous example of coastal erosion would surely have left some traces behind — as at Dunluce Castle in County Antrim. In fact the shore beneath Dún Aonghasa is among the clearest on the west coast of Inis Mór. Moreover, there are other semicircular cliff-edge forts in County Clare (at Cahercommaun and Caherlismacsheedy).

Today, at any rate, the inner citadel is a semicircle with a diameter of 150 feet. There is a middle enclosure, 400 x 300 feet, and an outer enclosure 1,175 x 650 feet which comprises about eleven acres. The middle wall is defended by an extensive *chevaux-de-frise*, a Frisian-style abatis here designed to withstand infantry attack — if one believes those who maintain that the fort was built after Aran had been denuded of its grassy coat. There is no doubt that today a cavalry charge against the fort would be unthinkable: the horses would break their legs in the crevices of the limestone plateau. The *chevaux-de-frise*, incidentally, is not unique to Dún Aonghasa: there is another Aran one at Dún Dúchathair and there are some on the mainland (e.g. Ballykinvarga, County Clare).

So much has been written in recent years about the links between archaeology and astronomy that I should like to raise a question here. Just as Newgrange in the Boyne valley is connected ceremoniously with the rising sun on midwinter's day, could Dún Aonghusa have been the focus of a ceremony on, say, midsummer's day, with tiers of prehistoric people gathered to watch the sun go down on Galway Bay?

Dún Dúchathair (The Black Fort) stands on the cliffs to the south of Dún Aonghasa and there is no doubt that some of the promontory on which it stands has fallen into the sea. Not only are there remains of the collapse visible in the ocean, but we have drawings of what it looked like before 1838 when a great storm tore away the remains of some rows of stone houses that had survived until a century before Father Browne photographed the fort.

The wall across the headland is approximately 200 feet long and averages twenty feet in height. The vestiges of some stone houses can be seen outside this wall. Inside, there are substantial remains of at least four oval houses, joined together for economy like terraced houses today.

Dún Eoghanachta (Dun Onaght) stands inland, on a limestone hill to the north-west of Dún Aonghasa and is quite different from the previous two in being almost circular. With an internal diameter of some ninety feet, the wall is over sixteen feet high and over thirteen feet wide at the base. This wall has a terrace below the parapet. One would think that this terrace, as at the other Aran forts, would give a clue to the date of construction (based on the average height of Irish skeletons through the millennia) but none of the experts I have consulted make mention of this.

Today there are nine sets of steps inside the fort, leading to the walkway and the parapet but opinions differ as to how many of these were added when the fort was restored in the 1880s. Also inside the fort are the remains of three rectangular stone houses. The largest of these has niches in the main wall, as can be seen in one of Father Browne's photographs.

A little over three miles east of Dún Eoghanachta, on the highest point of Inis Mór, stands the impressive fortress of **Dún Eochla** (Dun Oughill). The inner area is roughly oval in shape, with diameters of ninety-three feet and seventy-six feet approximately. For the most part, the wall is over sixteen feet high and twelve feet wide at the base. Again there is a terrace below the parapet of the wall and again there are many flights of steps, both straight and lateral, built into the wall. Apparently there were originally two terraces below the parapet of this fort, as can be seen in a sketch of the building, dated 1700, at the British Library, London.

An outer enclosure, roughly oval in shape, measures 250 x 200 feet. It is surrounded by another terraced wall nearly twenty feet high in places and nearly seventeen feet wide at the base. Before it was restored in the 1880s, there was only one set of steps leading to the walkway and it was the restorers who were responsible for what is today the most unusual feature of the fort, a drum-like stage in the inner enclosure that is prominent in one of Father Browne's photographs. The presumption is that the stage was built from stones, lying loose in the interior, which had originally been the walls of circular or rectangular houses like the ones at Dún Dúchathair and Dún Eoghanachta respectively.

Dún Chonchúir (Dun Conor) on Inis Meáin has been described as the most magnificent ring fort in the whole of Ireland. The bailey or outer enclosure is oval in shape and measures 230 x 115 feet internally. It surrounds a hilltop, using a rocky gully on one side for its outer defences. The inner fortress is likewise oval. Its great wall is still twenty feet high in places and is over eighteen feet thick at the base. Its diameters are 225 and 115 feet. Originally, this wall had two terraces. Today it has three terraces in some places due to faulty reconstruction in the last century when the outside walls were also buttressed as at Dún Aonghasa.

In the interior are the remains of seven *clocháns* or stone houses which are joined together against the inside wall as at Dún Dúchathair. Nobody knows who lived in these houses. Nobody knows even who Conor was for certain. Conor and Aengus have long since passed into the realm of legend unlike the early Christian saints of Aran whose churches we shall be examining shortly. This in itself suggests that the forts are a lot older than the churches, a speculation with which not every archaeologist agrees.

Beehive *clocháns* (i.e. stone houses built with successively overlapping flagstones) are commonplace in Ireland wherever there was suitable stone and little timber. On Aran, besides being built inside some forts, many of these were built separately on all three islands. **Clochán na Carraige** is the best known of these and is very well preserved. As Father Browne's photograph shows, the interior was as dry in 1938 as the day it was completed.

Externally, Clochán na Carraige is oval in shape, but inside it is a rectangle measuring nineteen *x* seven-and-a-half feet. It is eight feet high at the centre. The walls are over three feet thick and there is a small window in one wall. Opposing doorways, nearly four feet high, pierce the two longer walls. The *clochán* is situated on low ground on the road between Kilmurvey and Onaght. While some archaeologists suggest that it may be coeval with the latter's fort, others remind us that farmers on the Dingle peninsula are *still* building huts like this as outhouses.

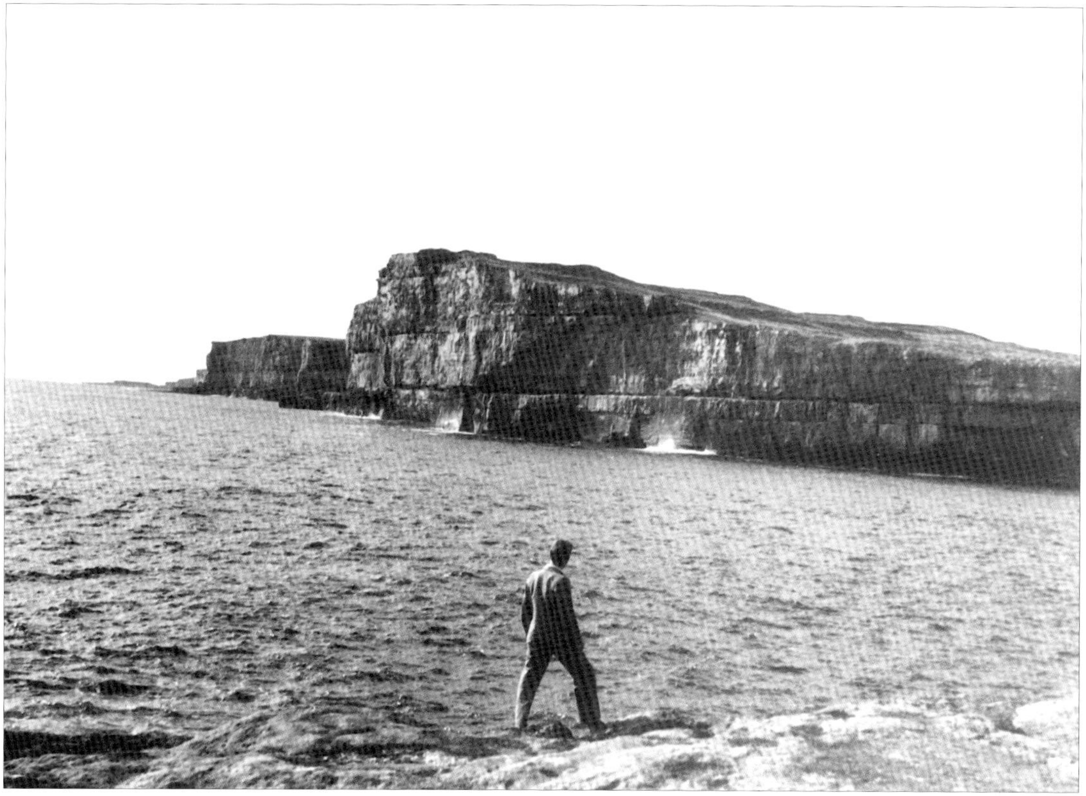

A tourist standing on Carraig na bPiseóg looks towards Ard na gCaorach with the majestic fort of Dún Aonghasa perched on the Clifftop.

A bird's eye view of Dún Aonghasa showing the massive encircling walls and the *chevaux-de-frise,* a Frisian-style defence-work made of sharp stones set in the ground.

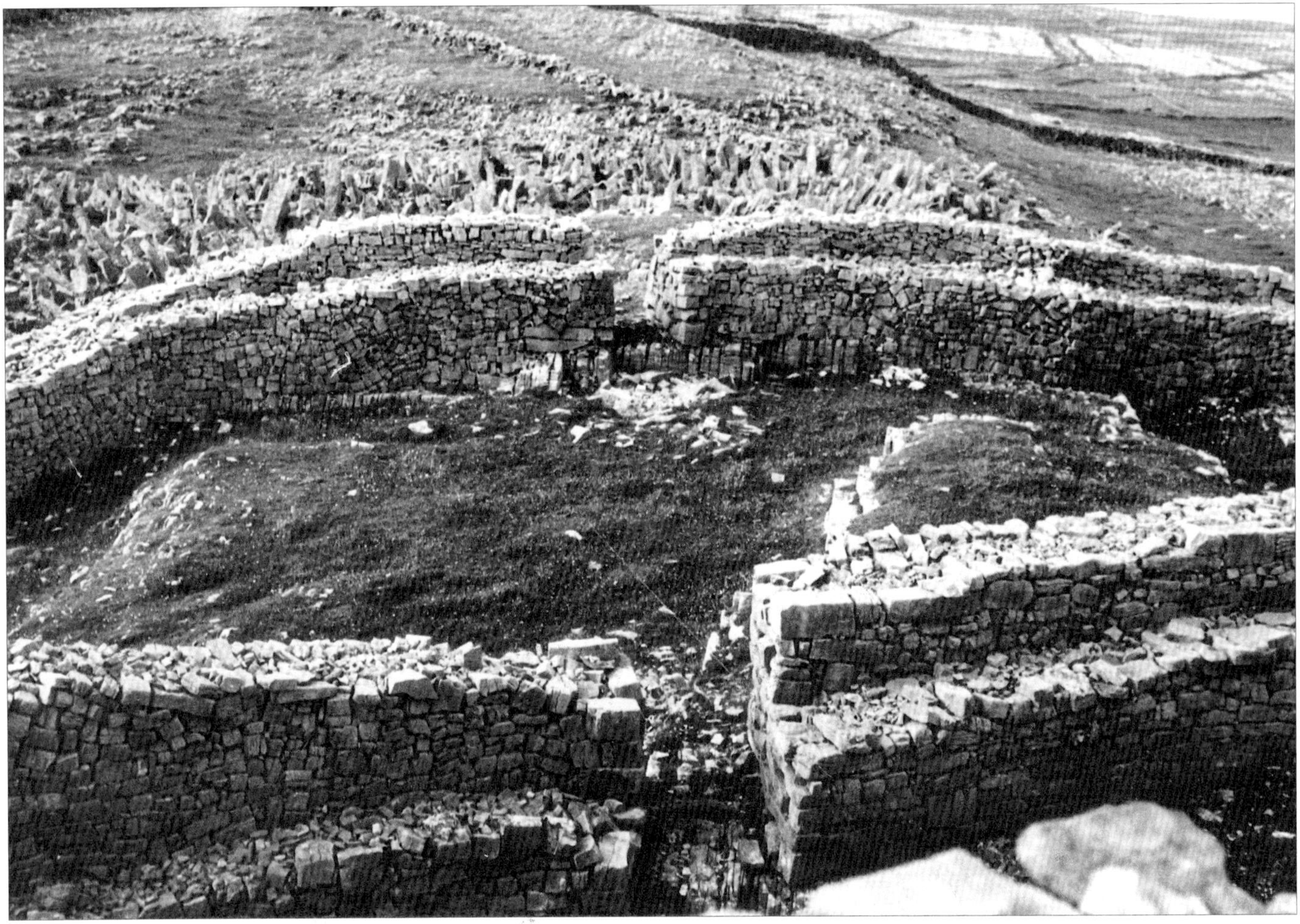

The Cliffs at Dún Dúchatair (the Black Fort) with Poll na Biscanagh in the foreground. The walls of the promontory fort itself can be seen on the left-hand side of the clifftop.

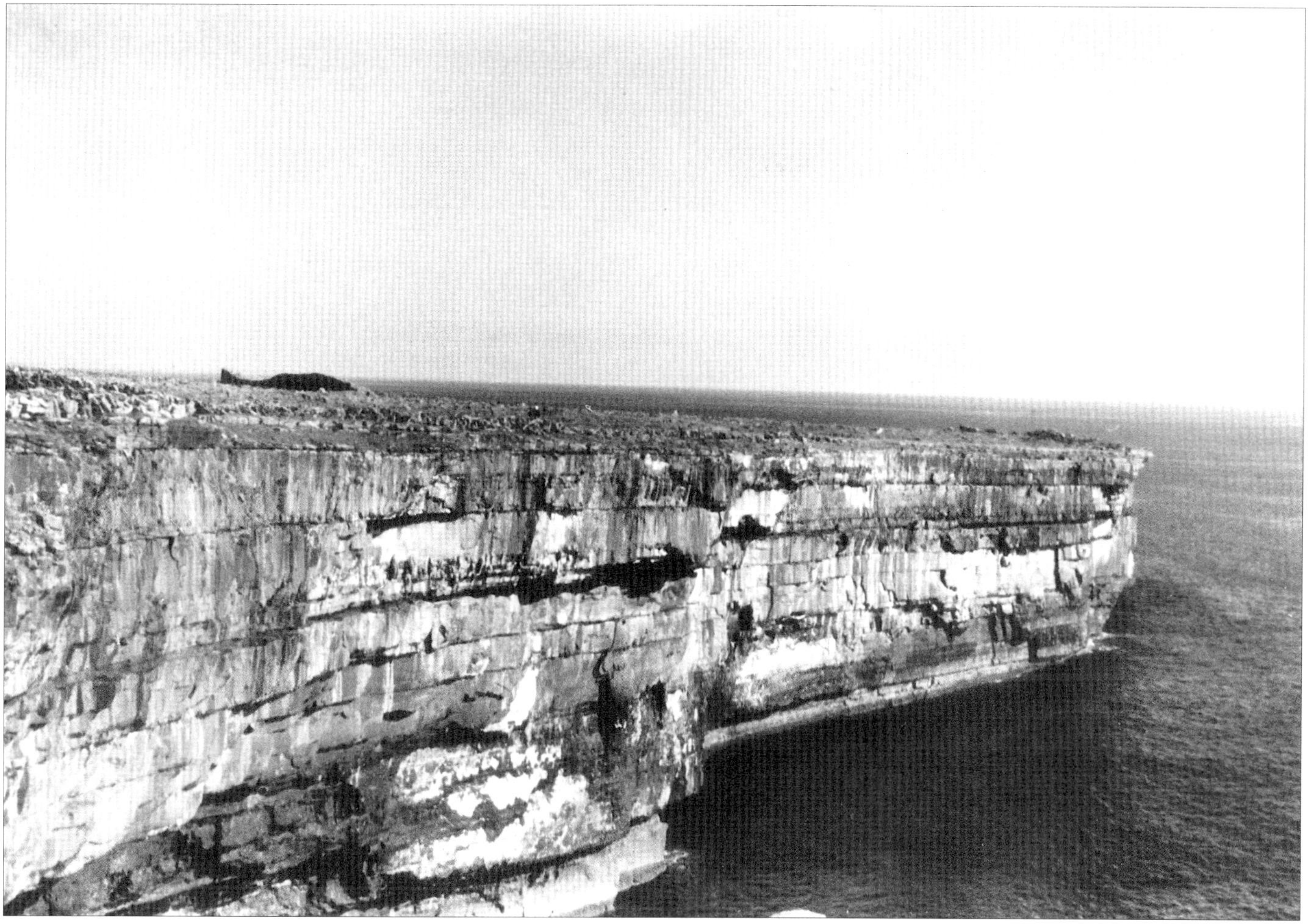

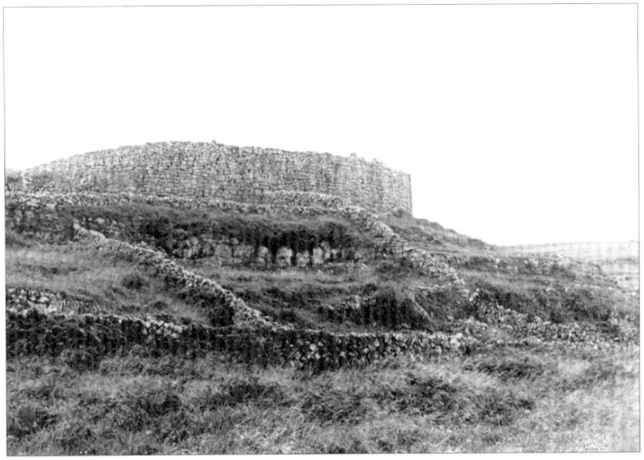

The exterior of the fort, Dún Eoghanachta (Dun Onaght). Not unlike Grianán of Aileach in County Donegal, its sixteen-feet-high hilltop wall presents a formidable obstacle to any would-be-attacker.

The interior of Dún Dúchathair showing the wall-walks under the parapet and the remains of the *clocháns* that were built inside the fort. They are reminiscent of the conjoined houses at Scara Brae in Orkney.

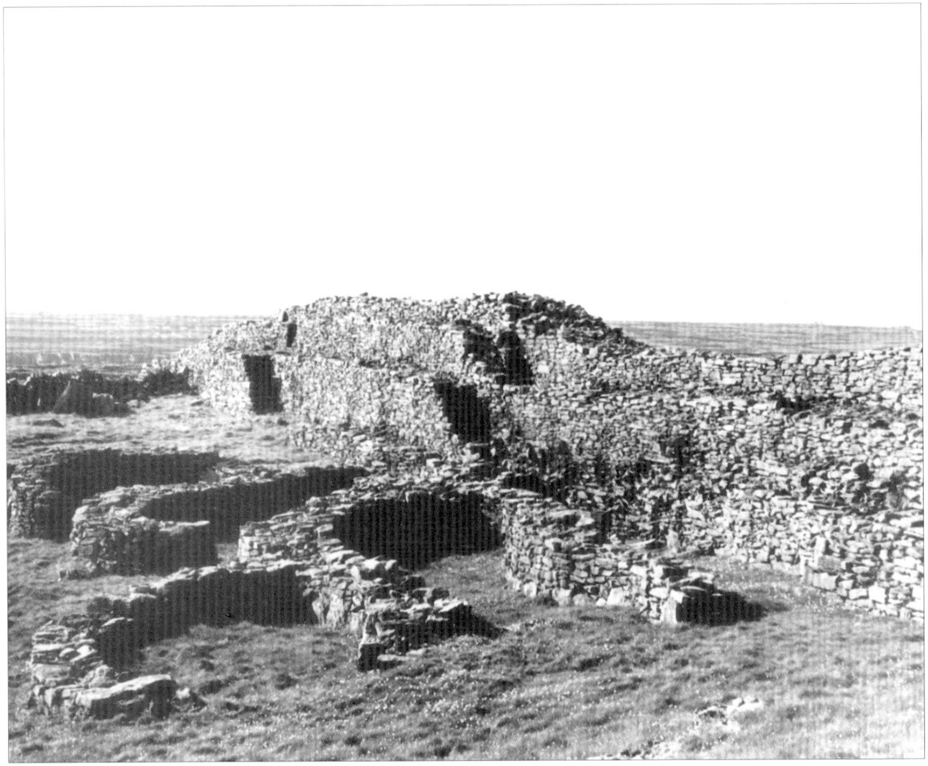

An interior wall at Dún Eoghanachta showing the origingal niches. Their original use has been the object of much contradictory speculation by archaeologists.

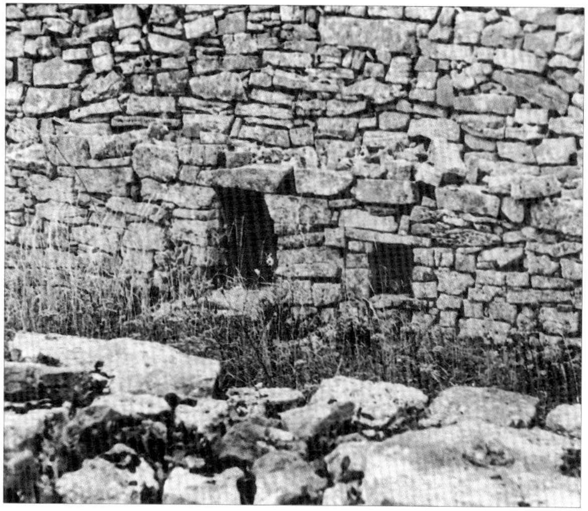

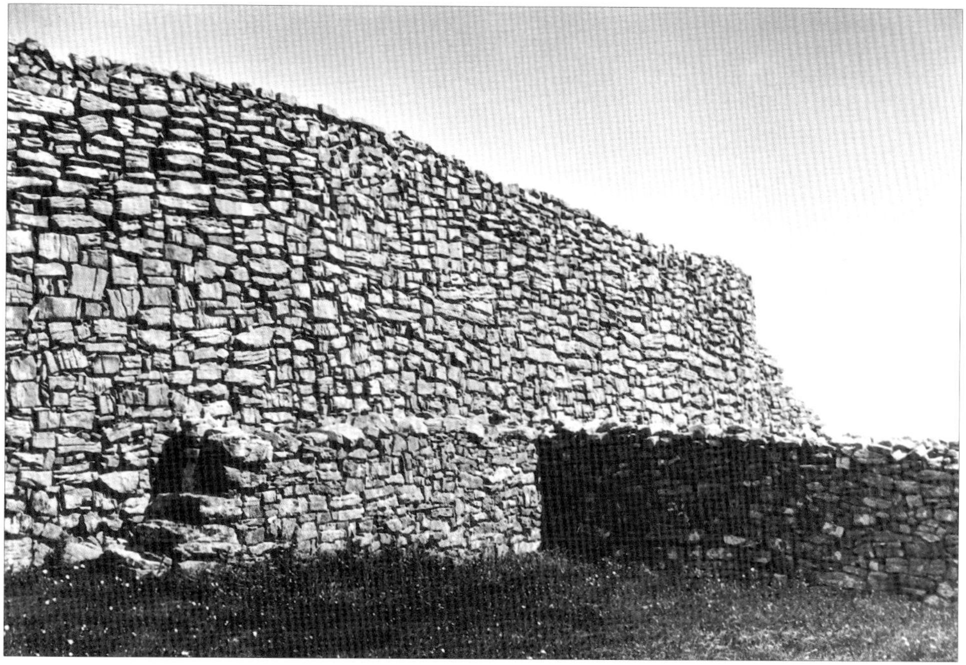

The outer wall of Dún Eochla (Dun Oughill) is over sixteen feet high and twelve feet wide at the base. The outer walkway may have been constructed during renovations in the last century. It is a glorified stile giving access to the next field.

The drum-like 'stage' inside Dún Eochla. Although this is the fort's most distinctive feature, it was built only in the 1880s when the restorers collected loose stones and gave them this formation.

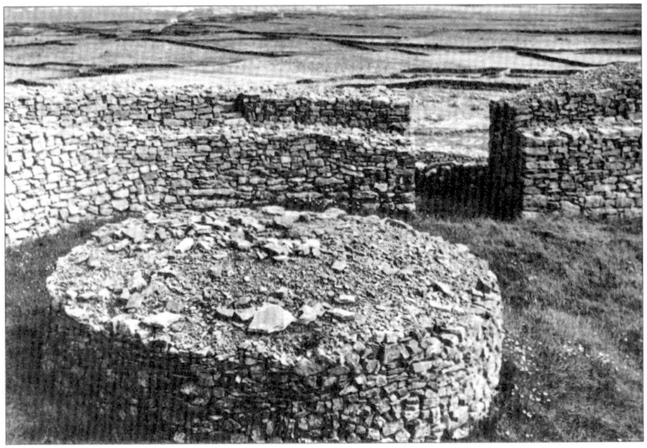

The rampart inside Dún Eochla showing its terrace and two sets of original steps. The fort is built on the highest point of Inis Mór (406 feet) so the view is commanding.

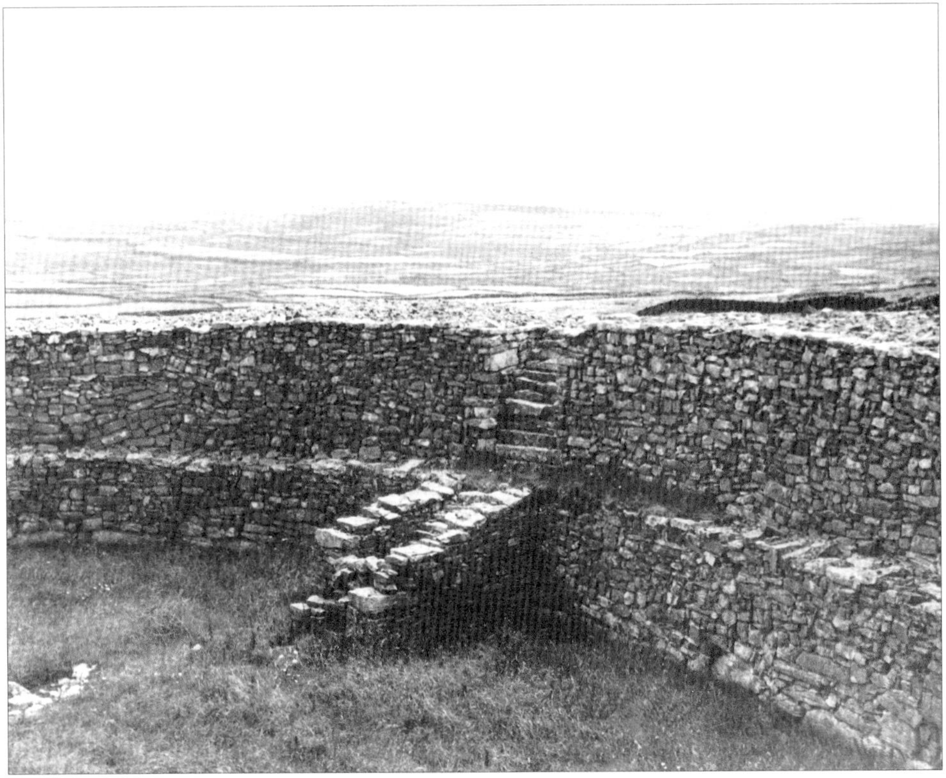

Exterior of the rampart at Dún Chonchúir (Dun Conor). This is the fort that dominates Inis Meáin. Its twenty-feet-high wall is the highest of any in Aran and the building has been described as "the most magnificent ring fort in the whole of Ireland".

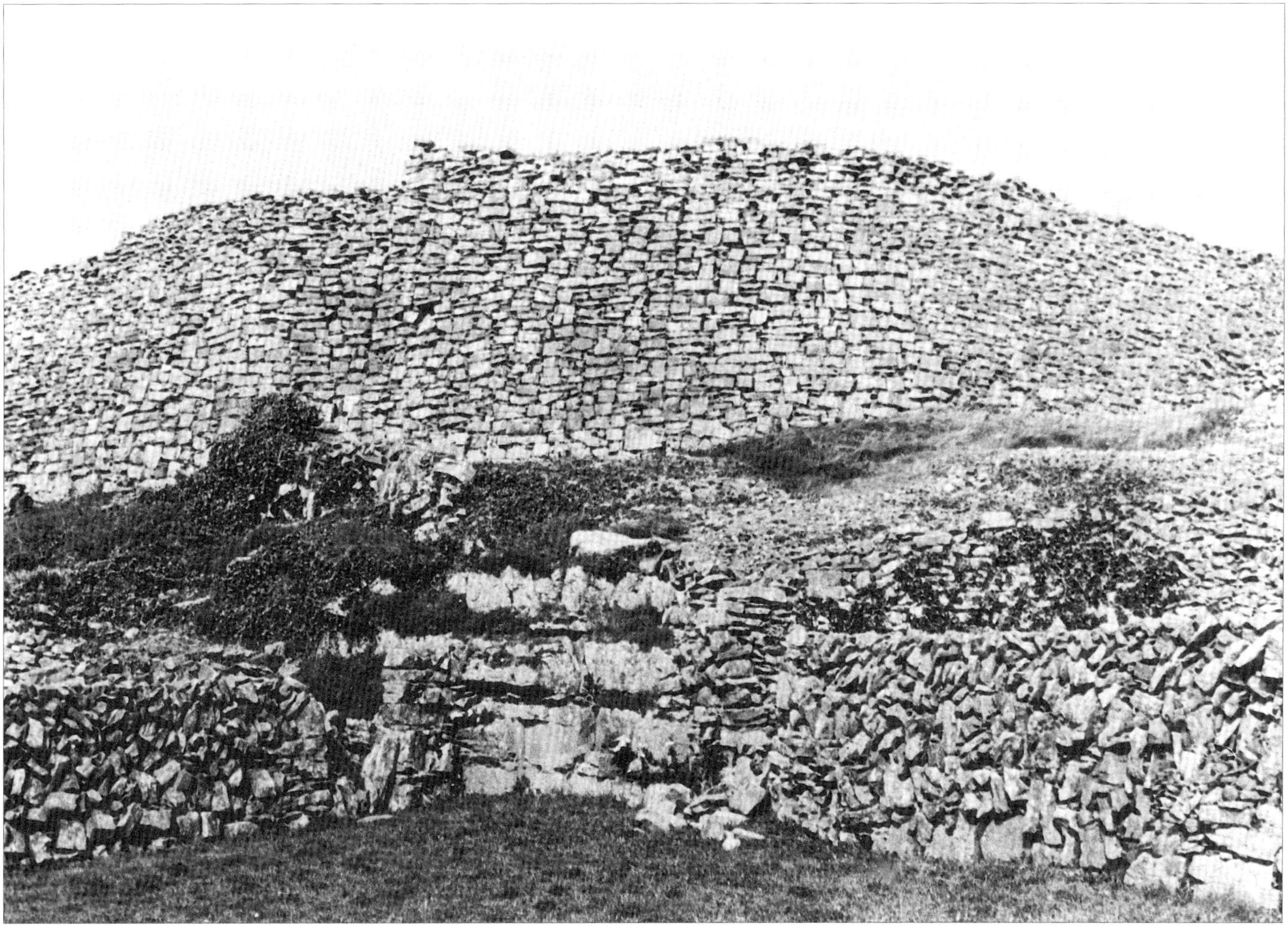

The interior of Dún Chonchúir showing the three terraces and the remains of seven *clocháns*, stone houses that were built against the inside wall.

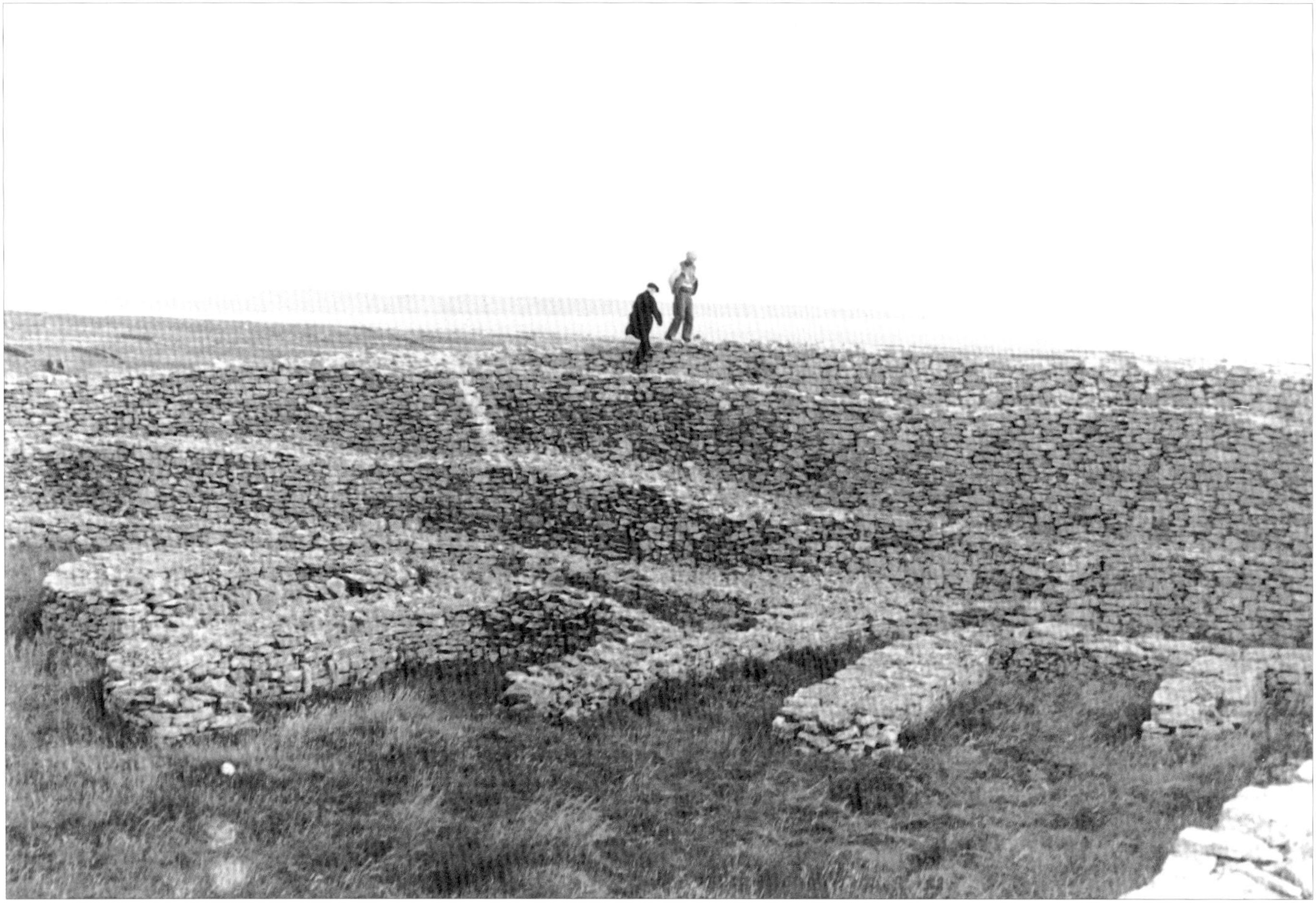

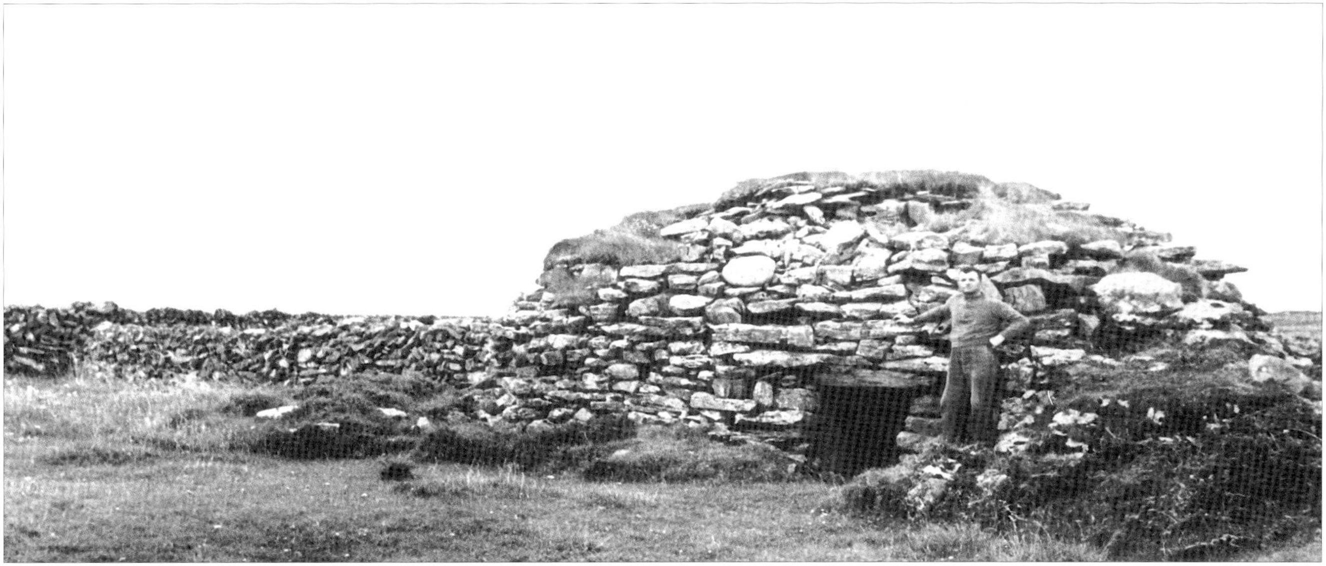

Above: We have seen several unroofed *clocháns* so far. Here is a fine example of a complete one, Clochán na Carraige. The house itself is eight feet high, the doorway being half that height. The corballed structure recalls the earlier Newgrange tomb in County Meath and the beehive huts of Skellig Rock off the coast of Kerry, built at later date.

Right: The interior of Clochán na Carraige showing the successively overlapping flagstones. The building is circular inside but rectangular outside.

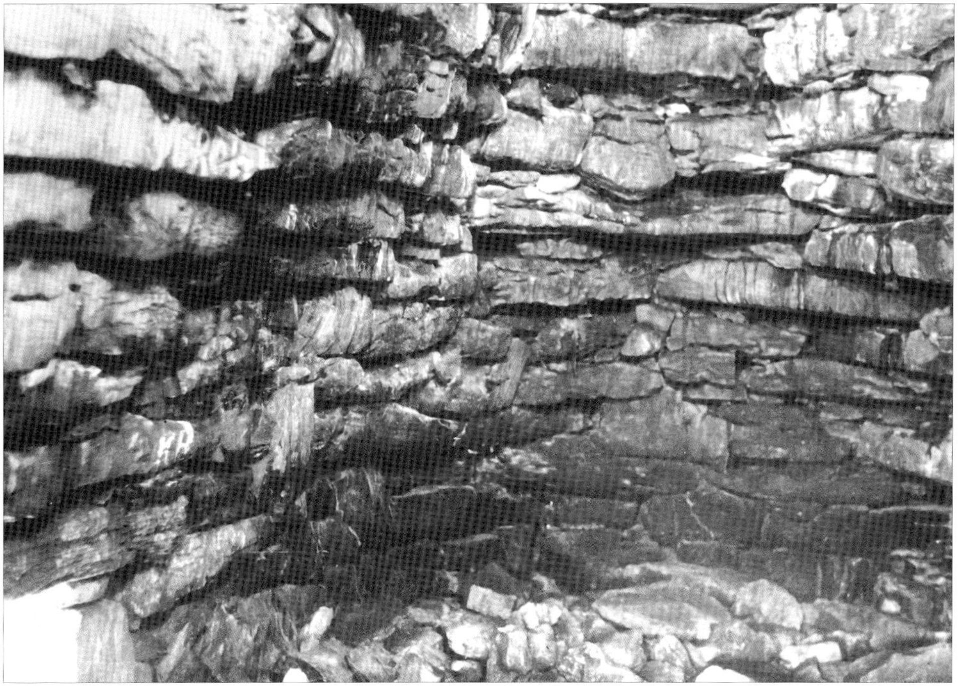

The 'Riders to the Sea' at Port na Mainistreach on Inis Mór are the Flaherty brothers, Colman and Gerard. The shoreline here is much higher today and a wall has been built to protect the road from the ocean.

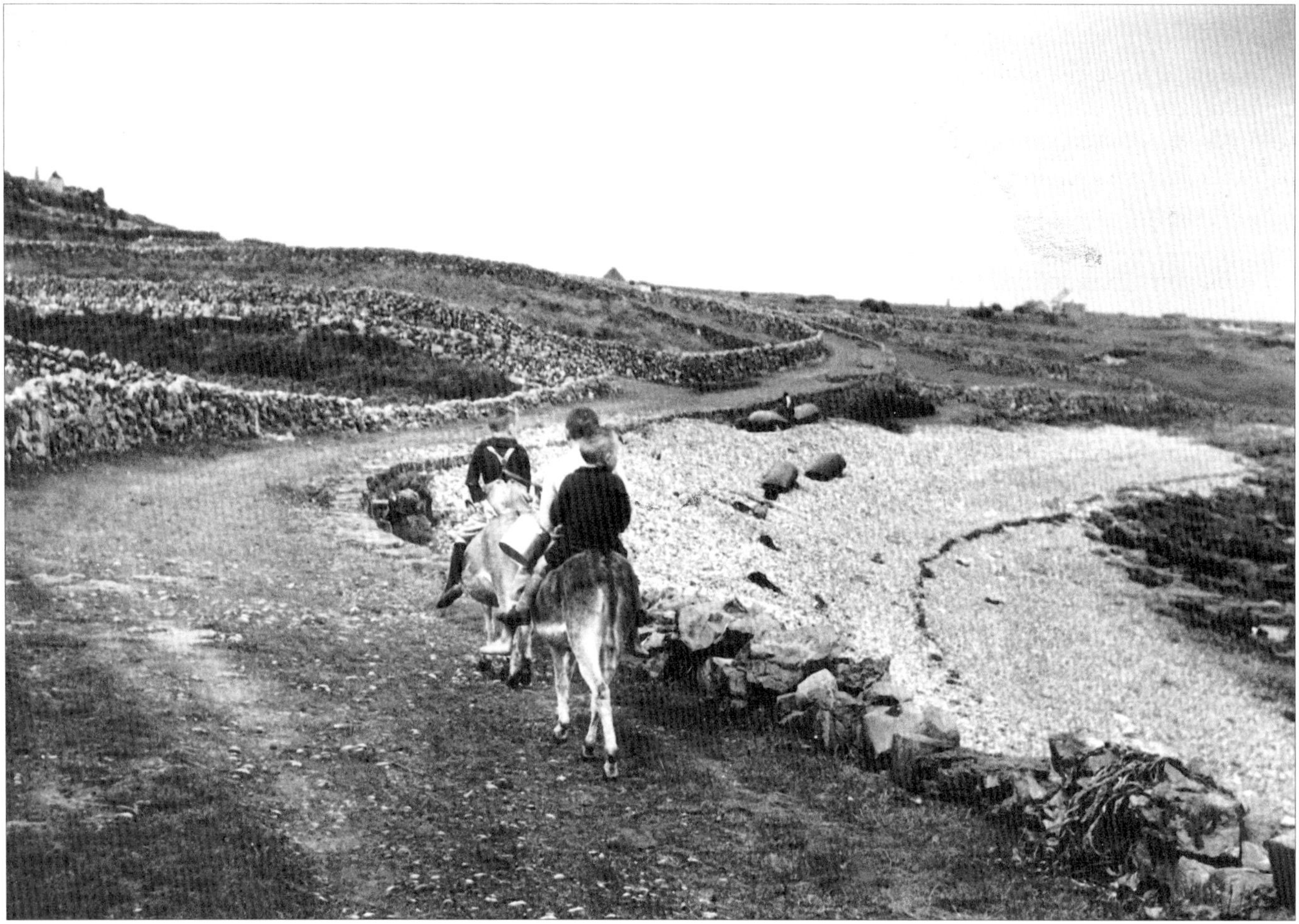

Chapter II

Boats & Currachs

Aran currachs are the successors of the prehistoric skin-covered rowing or sailing craft that brought the first settlers to these islands about five thousand years ago. One of Father Browne's photographs shows how they are made.

The materials used in 1938 — and still in use today — were quite different from earlier days. Instead of building the framework from local wood, the ribs tied with thongs of sallies and covered with cowskins, the islanders now use imported woods, mainly white spruce, copper nails and new canvas that comes in bales. The gunwale is made first. Then, as shown in this chapter, the currach-to-be is turned upside down and placed on crates. (No doubt, plastic cola crates have replaced the wooden ones seen here.) The main ribs and cross-members are fitted to make an open-work frame. This is then covered with canvas and given several liberal coatings of tar. If a currach is holed, whether by a rock or a calf's foot, it is easy to repair. A patch of canvas is ironed on with hot tar and the boat is seaworthy once more.

As can be seen here, the currach is keel-less and rudder-less. Its navigation depends on oars and ballast. The oars are bladeless, long and narrow. They pivot on thole-pins that pass through holes in wooden lugs on the shafts of the oars. The ballast consists of carefully-chosen beach boulders.

Currachs have two to four oarsmen and nowadays often carry an outboard motor. In Father Browne's day such a luxury was unheard of. The currach is a notably safe vessel that can ride even the roughest seas like a storm petrel. In his film, *Man of Aran* (1934), Robert Flaherty showed currachs thriving in the fifty-foot waves that raced through Brannock Sound at the western end of Inis Mór.

Before the advent of modern trawlers, Father Browne was able to photograph the Connemara hookers and their smaller sisters — known as *pucáns* — which were two of the finest small sailing boats ever built for fishing.

With black hulls and brown sails they could fairly speed through the water. Their broad bellies let them sit in the sea like ocean ducks, and even in rough weather they were remarkably safe. A few still exist, although they are now a tourist attraction and a magnet for sailing enthusiasts. Besides being used for fishing, the Connemara boats were used as Aran freighters. For many decades they carried turf from the mainland — a fuel now replaced by bottled gas.

Larger than the hooker was the two-masted 'nobby' (or Aran ketch) which was basically a freighter-cum-trawler that plied between the islands and from the islands to Galway, thirty miles away. The 'nobby' would often be chartered to transport groups of tourists who wished to visit all three islands during their visit. Interestingly it is a hooker, not a 'nobby', that is carrying the group of Navan boys and their bicycles to the mainland from Kilronan in Father Browne's photograph here.

At the beginning and end of this book we see photographs taken aboard the *Dun Aengus,* the Dublin-built steamer operated by the Galway Bay Steamship Company and subsequently by Córas Iompair Éireann, the state transport company, which took it over in 1951. For forty-six years, between 1912 and 1958, the *Dun Aengus* carried passengers, livestock and freight between Galway and the islands. At Kilronan on Inis Mór she was able to dock, but at the other two islands she had to off-load into currachs, a problematical operation when cattle, horses or elderly ladies were in question. The first piers to be built on Inis Meáin and Inis Oírr were completed in 1997.

In 1958 the *Dun Aengus* was replaced by the *Naomh Éanna*, also Dublin-built, and in due course she has been replaced by a multiple service of smaller vessels from Rossaveal and Doolin as well as from Galway City.

Below: A Connemara hooker bringing turf from the mainland of County Galway to Inis Mór.

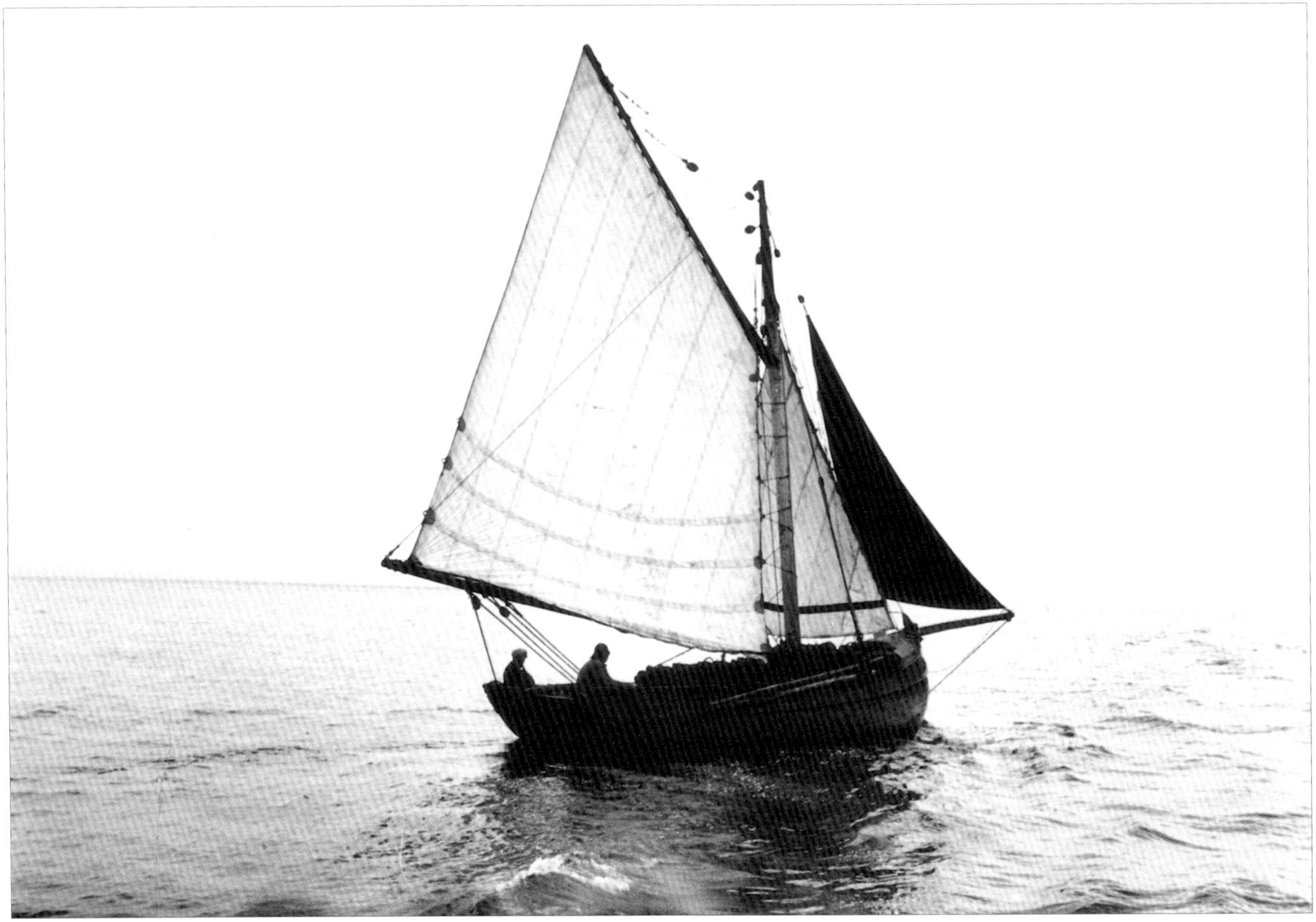

Aran trawlers at Galway (1925). European Community fishing restrictions have adversely affected the fishing-fleet of Aran today. Nevertheless, the industry nowadays — as in Father Browne's day — provides the islands with their most stable income.

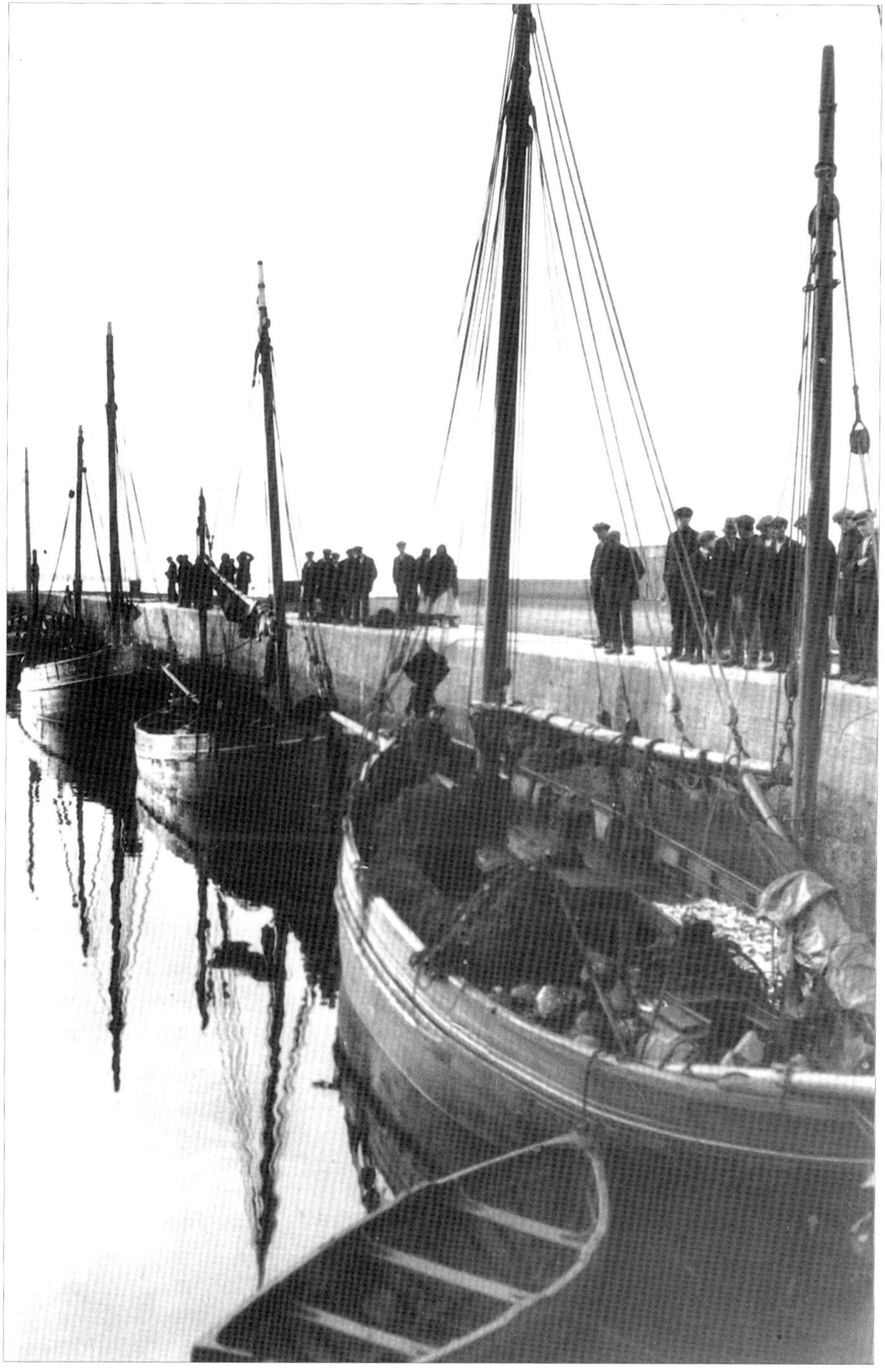

A two-masted 'nobby' with zulu stern pictured off Inis Oírr. The 'nobby' was an efficient Aran ketch that acted as both trawler and freighter.

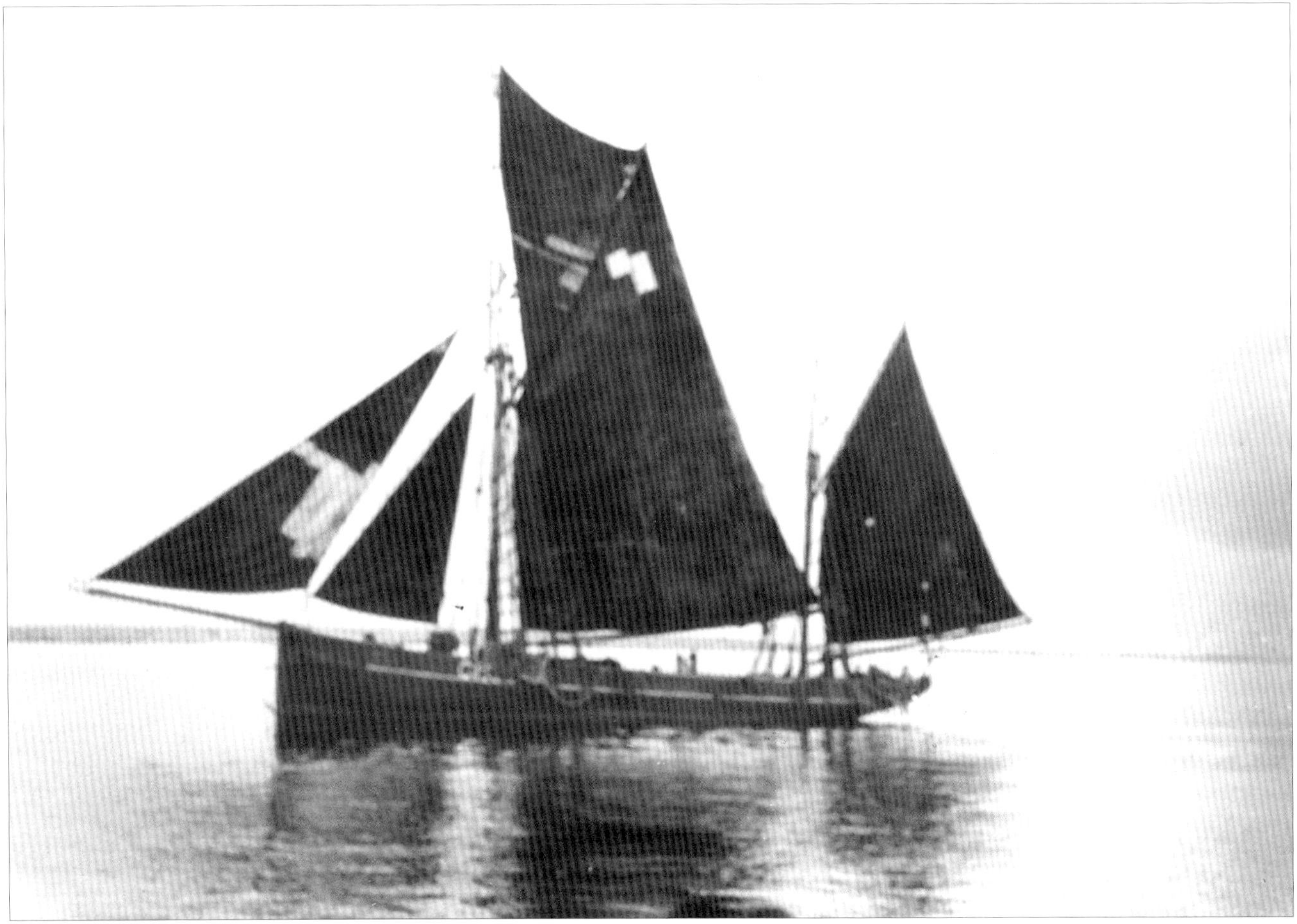

A group of boys from Navan, County Meath, leaving Kilronan pier in a Connemara hooker. They had spent the summer improving their Irish and are being helped to board by Pádraig Dirrane of Kilronan.

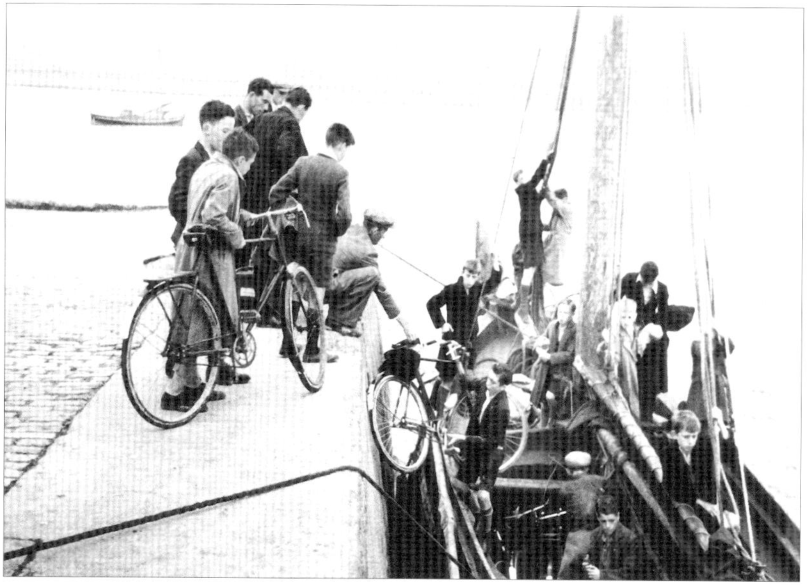

Killeany Harbour, with the town of Kilronan in the background. The two-masted 'nobby' belongs to Pat Fitzpatrick, and Pat Gill's Connemara 'half-boat' is in the foreground. The pier and the wall behind it are now concreted. The stone beacons in the bay are the same today but two new lighted buoys have been added nearer to the shore.

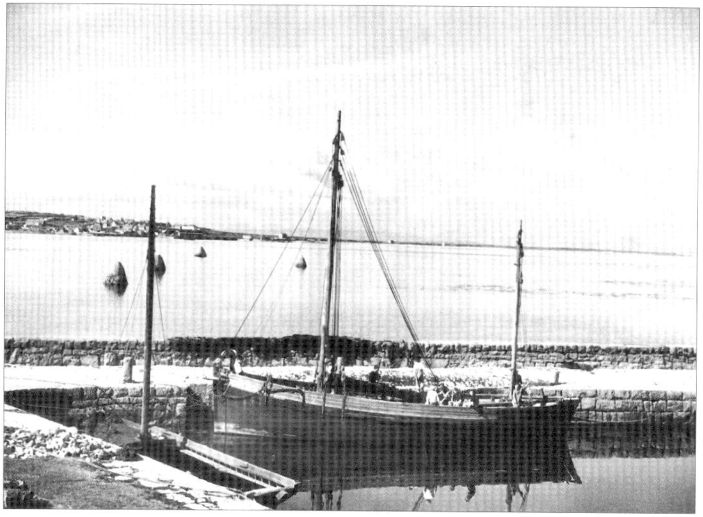

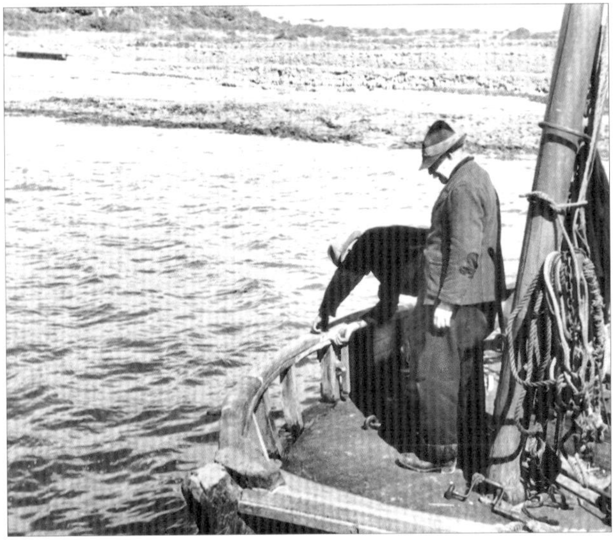

Patrick and Robert Gill mending their Connemara hooker at Kilronan on Inis Mór.

Below: Tommy O'Donnell's currach in the course of construction at Kilronan. The mode of manufacture is explained in the preamble to this chapter.

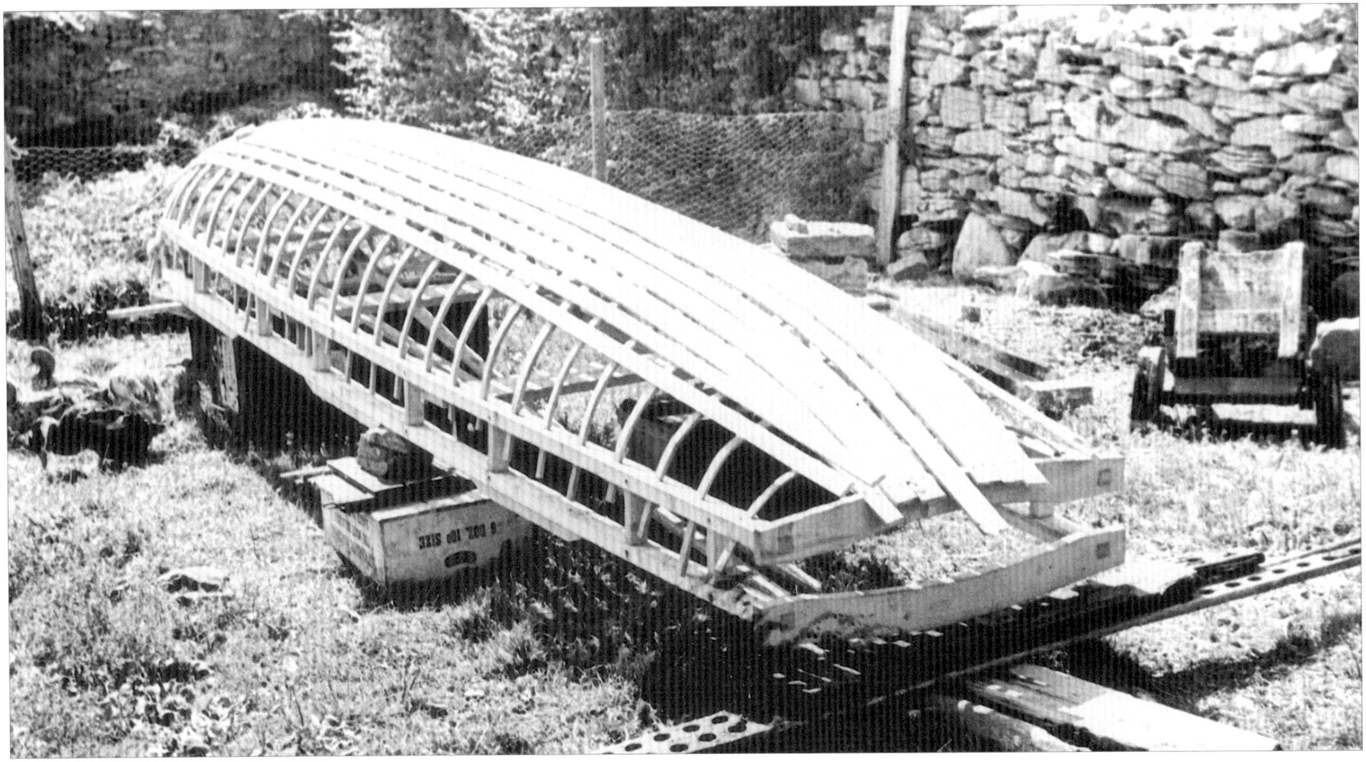

Currachs from Trácht Each on Inis Oírr crossing the Foul Sound to Inis Meáin. The headland on the left is Ceann an Bhrúgh. (1925)

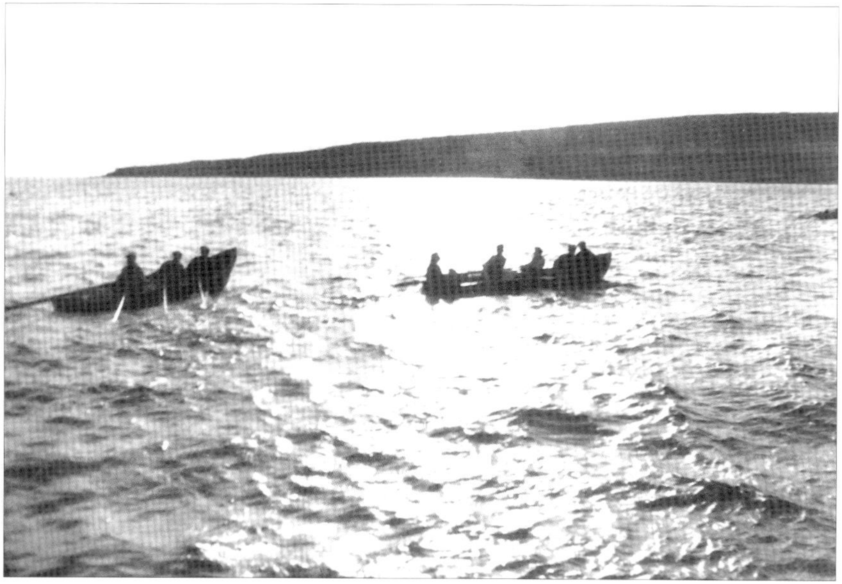

Upturned currach at Port na Mainistreach. The boy facing the camera is Michael Johnny Mhichil Conneely.

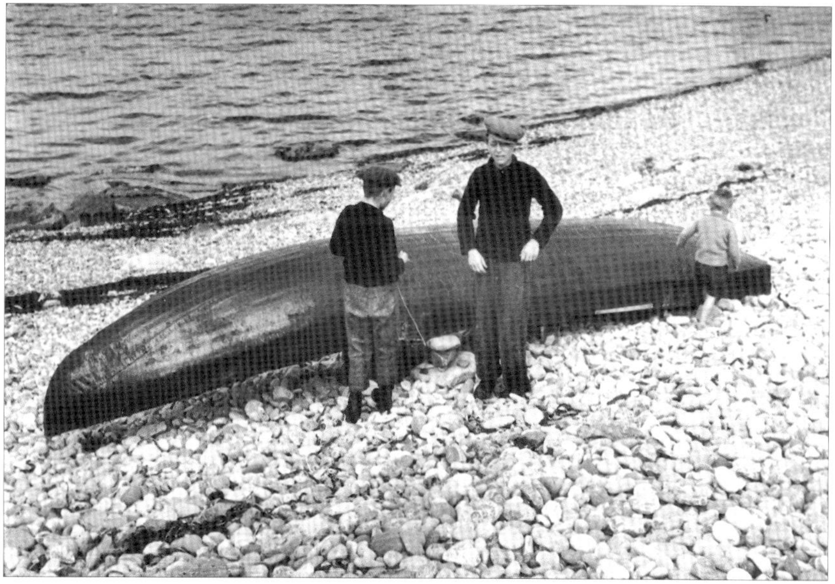

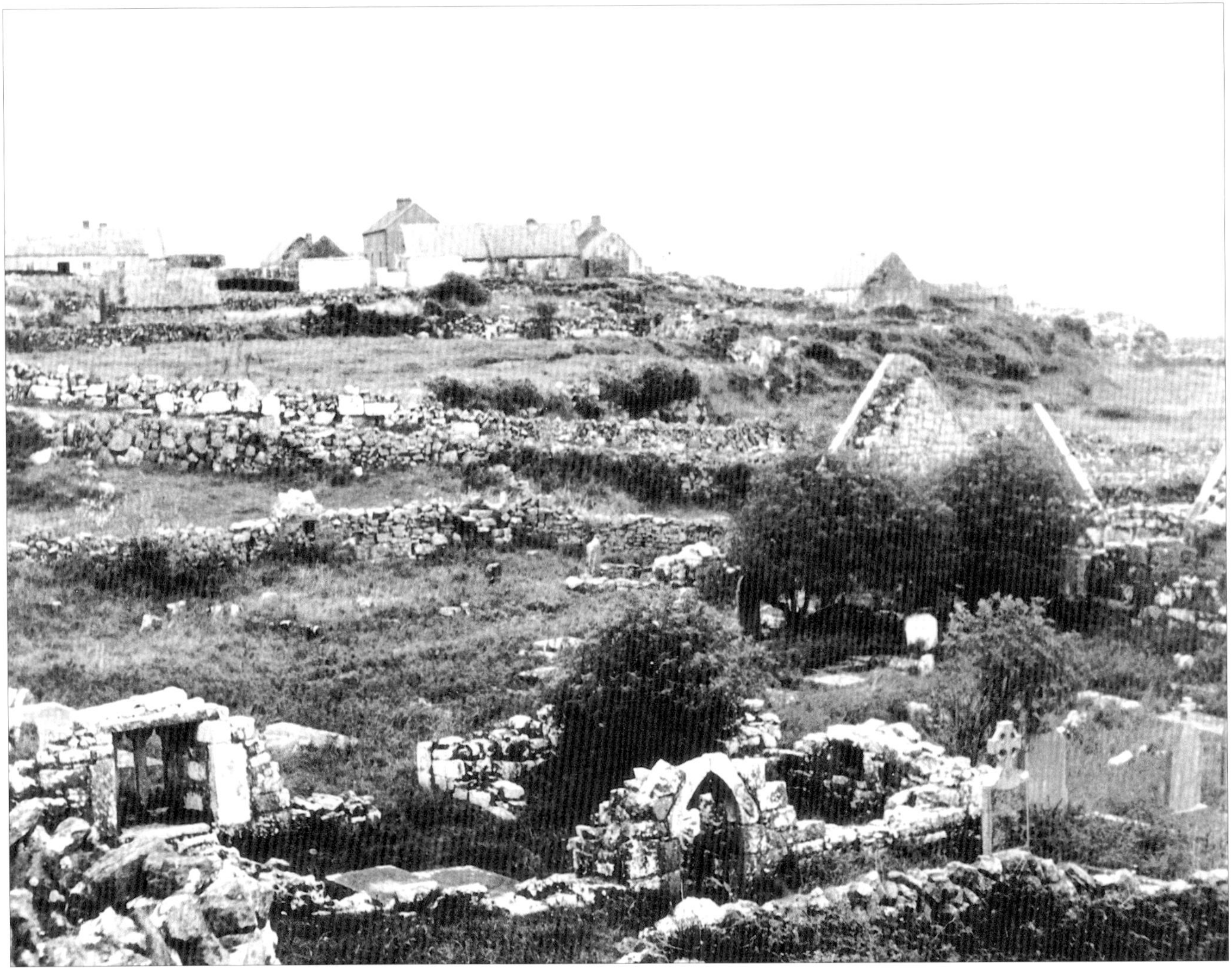

Overview of na Seacht dTeampaill (The Seven Churches). There are only two churches at this ancient monastic site, Teampall an Phoill (in the foreground) and Teampall Bhreacáin (at the right). The houses on the skyline, Flahertys', Dirranes' and Hernons', are still standing.

Chapter III

Monastic & Religious Aran

Given his profession, it is hardly surprising to hear that Father Browne devoted much of his time on Aran to photographing the numerous ruined churches and monasteries. The remains of these buildings are dotted throughout the islands, the earliest of them dating back almost to the time of St Enda (Naomh Éinne) who is said to have died in 520 A.D.

The islanders have forgotten all about Aengus and Conor, as we have seen, but they still know a lot about the men and women who gave their islands the name "Ára na Naomh", Aran of the Saints. In Father Browne's time, they were still building a church which would have stained glass windows in honour of Saints Enda, Brecan and Cavan.

Before the British turned Kilronan into the capital of the islands in the sixteenth century, the most important place in Aran was Killeany, or in Irish, Cill Éinne. Here the church of St Enda was the focal point of the monastery which he founded on Inis Mór. The main church and other monastic buildings were demolished by Cromwell's army in the 1650s; their stones went into the rebuilding of nearby Arkyn Castle. The fragments of the High Cross of Killeany which Father Browne photographed were once incorporated into the walls of this castle.

St Enda's foundation was one of the principal monasteries of Ireland. It is reputed to have been visited by Saints Columcille, Brendan and Kieran before they went on to found their own houses at Derry, Clonfert and Clonmacnois respectively. But since nothing of the monastery remained to be photographed, Father Browne turned his attention to the next most important monastic settlement on Inis Mór. This was called, in English, "The Seven Churches".

The complex of buildings known in Irish as **na Seacht dTeampaill** stands near the village of Onaght at the western end of Inis Mór. The name is a misnomer which calls for some explanation. Up to the fifteenth century, when a second church was added to the complex, there was only one church here. It was called **Teampall Bhreacáin,** St Brecan's Church. I suggest that the original name was "The Church of the Seven (Requests)", not "The Seven Churches". A fifteenth century poem puts these words into the mouth of St Brecan: "I was granted my seven requests. God was satisfied with my offerings, not least of them being that on an enclosed piece of land He created a sanctuary for pilgrims."

The same poem tells us that before he came to Aran, where he destroyed a pagan idol and took its name, Brecan, the saint's name was Bresal and he was the son of Eochaidh, king of the Dál Cais of Clare, who ruled at the end of the fifth century. It is not too farfetched to suggest that Inis Mór was once named after this princely saint and known in Norse as Hy Brazil, the island of Bresal.

Teampall Bhreacáin is a large building, now assigned to the eighth century, which stands near the saint's grave. The building was nearly doubled in size during the tenth century when a chancel was added. The lines of the original gable end can still be seen in the western gable. The original doorway was in the south wall.

Up to the fifteenth century, the rest of the buildings in this complex were domestic buildings for the monks and for the many pilgrims, lay and religious, who visited this monastery every year. Some of them are of a late medieval date, proving that this was a venerated place for many centuries.

The church that was added in the fifteenth century is called **Teampall an Phoill** (The Church of the Hollow). It is a simple, rectangular church with a Gothic arch over the door and a Gothic window in one of the gable ends. The church stands in a graveyard that has many inscribed stones. One of these is said to read "TOMAS AP", a reference to St Thomas the Apostle. It would make more sense if it read "TOMAS AB" and marked the grave of a former abbot of the monastery. Another stone is marked "VII ROMANI". This has been the object of many interpretations which range from a reference to the Roman versus Celtic dispute — over the date of Easter — to a reference to seven pilgrims who had been to Rome. A suggestion I have not seen anywhere is that it may refer to Chapter Seven of St Paul's letter to the Romans which says (in verse six): "Now we are dead to that which held us captive."

The next church that Father Browne photographed was **Teampall an Ceathrar Álainn.** "The Church of the Four Beautiful Ones" is the normal translation of this name, the "beautiful ones" being St Brendan of Birr, and Saints Fursey, Conall and Berchan. Personally, I find it hard to believe that the church is dedicated to such a disparate group. It would make more sense to me if the "Álainn" of the title referred to "students" or even "Leinstermen": in rish these sound similar and could easily have been mistranslated through the course of centuries in oral tradition. The church itself resembles Teampall an Phoill but lacks its Gothic elements despite being assigned to the fifteenth century.

Then we come to **Teampall Mac Duagh,** dedicated to the founder of the monastery of Kilmacduagh in County Galway. This was built in at least two stages, as can be seen clearly in Father Browne's photograph. The earlier, eleventh century part is built of very large stones, while the later, thirteenth century chancel almost doubled the size of the building which stands near the village of Kilmurvey.

Mainistir Chiaráin, the monastery of St Kieran, is supposed to have been founded in the sixth century before that saint went on to establish his more famous monastery at Clonmacnois. Quite a few monuments remain here, the most substantial being the church. It is a well-preserved medieval building with a square doorway at the west end and an unusual window at the east end. This window shows Romanesque architecture (with its rounded arch) giving way to Gothic (with pointed arch and distinctive mouldings). The window is widely splayed on the inside, as can be seen in the picture Father Browne took from a vantage-point on the west.

From here the photographer retraced his steps and climbed up to **Teampall Bheanáin** which stands on a magnificent site that on a clear day gives wonderful views of the mainland. St Benan's Church, as it is called in English, is said to be the oldest church still standing on Aran. Of fifth-century date, it is dedicated to the saint who succeeded St Patrick at Armagh in 461 A.D. Built of massive stones, the church is unique in Aran because it is oriented north-south, rather that the normal east-west. Opinions differ as to whether this was due to the lie of the land or because of its windswept position.

Also built of massive stones is the rectangular church known as **Teaglach Éinne** which stands in St Enda's graveyard at the eastern end of Inis Mór. Like some of the other churches that Father Browne photographed, this one was built in two stages: the eastern half dates back to the ninth century, and during the seventeenth century the building was extended westwards by about ten feet and a new window and doorway were opened in the north wall.

On Inis Meáin, near the landing slip at Cora Point, Father Browne took an interesting set of pictures at **Cill Chennannach.** The "Church of the Canons" — one possible translation of its name — is situated in a rectangular graveyard paved with nineteenth century slab tombstones. Certainly erected by the end of the tenth century, the church is built of large stones and has walls two feet thick. It has projecting cobels which are a rare feature on early Irish churches.

Apart from the churches, Aran is full of other religious remains such as its holy wells, cross-slabs, and inscribed cenotaphs. This chapter includes examples of each of these. Pride of place is given to the High Cross of Aran. Three pieces of this had been cemented together and were photographed by Father Browne in Teaglach Éinne where they can still be seen.

To give a sense of the continuity of Christian tradition on Aran, the chapter concludes with a photograph of a church still in the course of construction. Being built on Inis Meáin is the beautiful **Teampall Mhuire** dedicated to Our Lady and replacing a fifteenth century church of the same name that had fallen down.

Aran retains its religious traditions and still has pilgrimages which are especially well-attended on 15 August in honour of the Blessed Virgin and on 9 June in honour of St Colmcille, the saint who must often have thought of Aran when he went to build his own island monastery on Iona.

Overview of na Seacht dTeampaill showing the historic graveyard where Saint Brecan, the founder of the monastery, is buried. His church, Teampaill Bhreacáin, is in the centre of the picture.

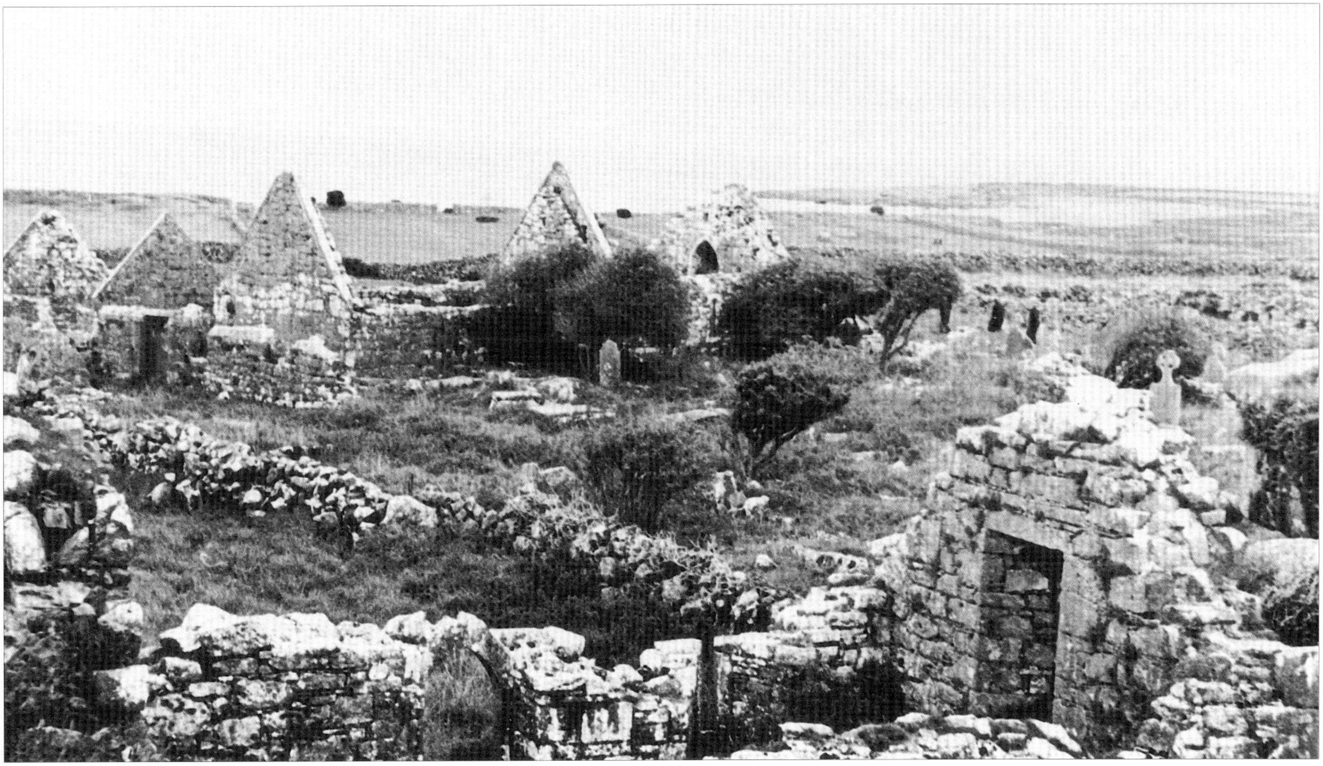

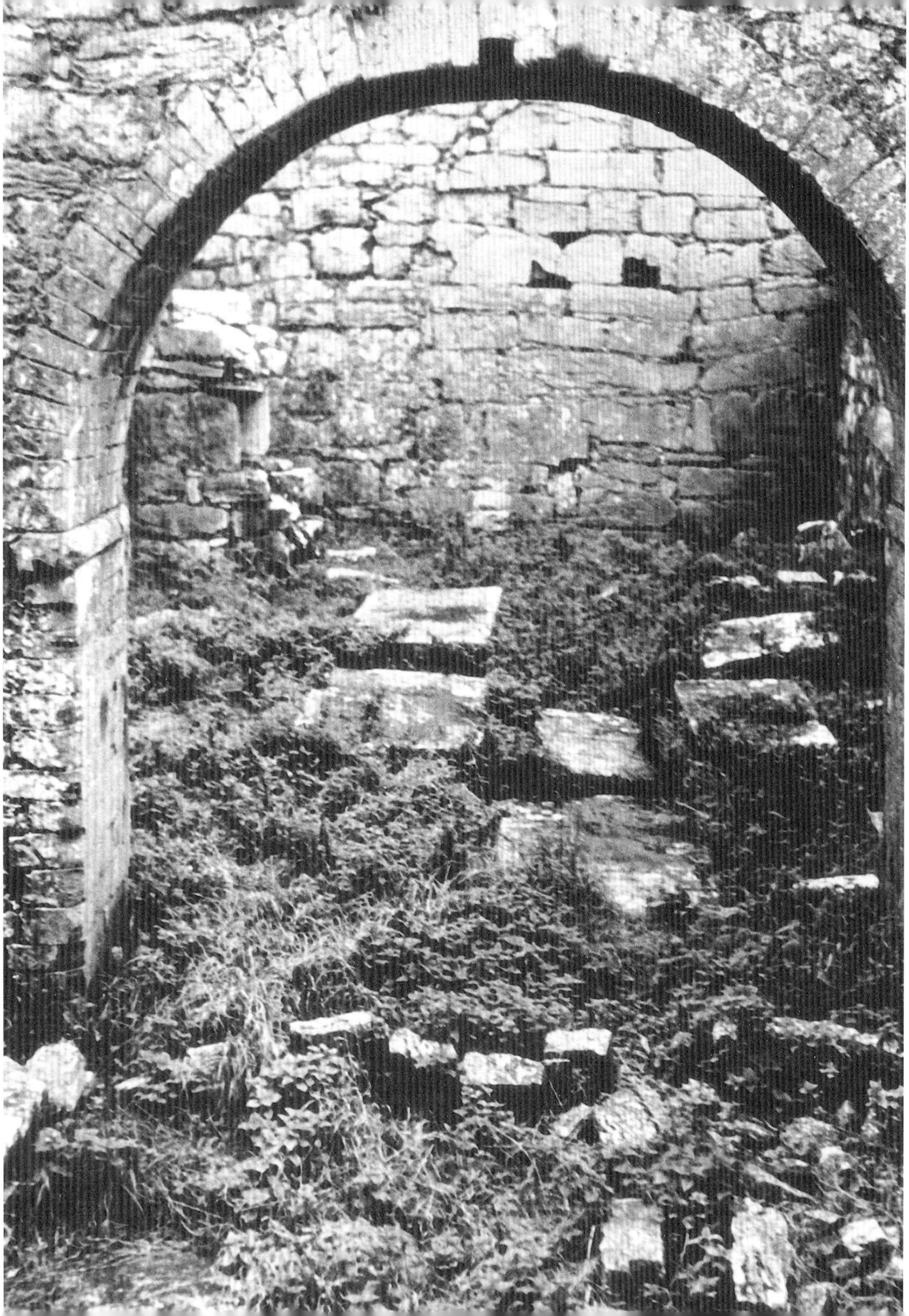

Facing page: Interior of Teampall Bhreacáin showing the chancel arch that was added when the size of this fifth century church was doubled five centuries later.

Right: Teampall an Phoill, the Church of the Hollow, at na Seacht dTeampaill. There is a Gothic doorway in the foreground and the foliage on the right conceals a Gothic window.

Below: Teampall an Ceathrar Álainn, where a pilgrimage is still held on 15 August. The houses on the right have now been demolished but the others, Concannons' and Donoghues', still stand.

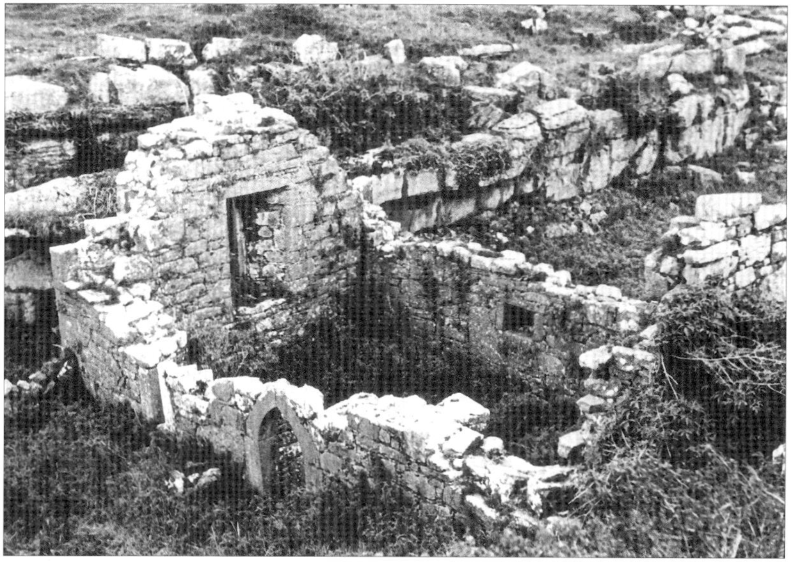

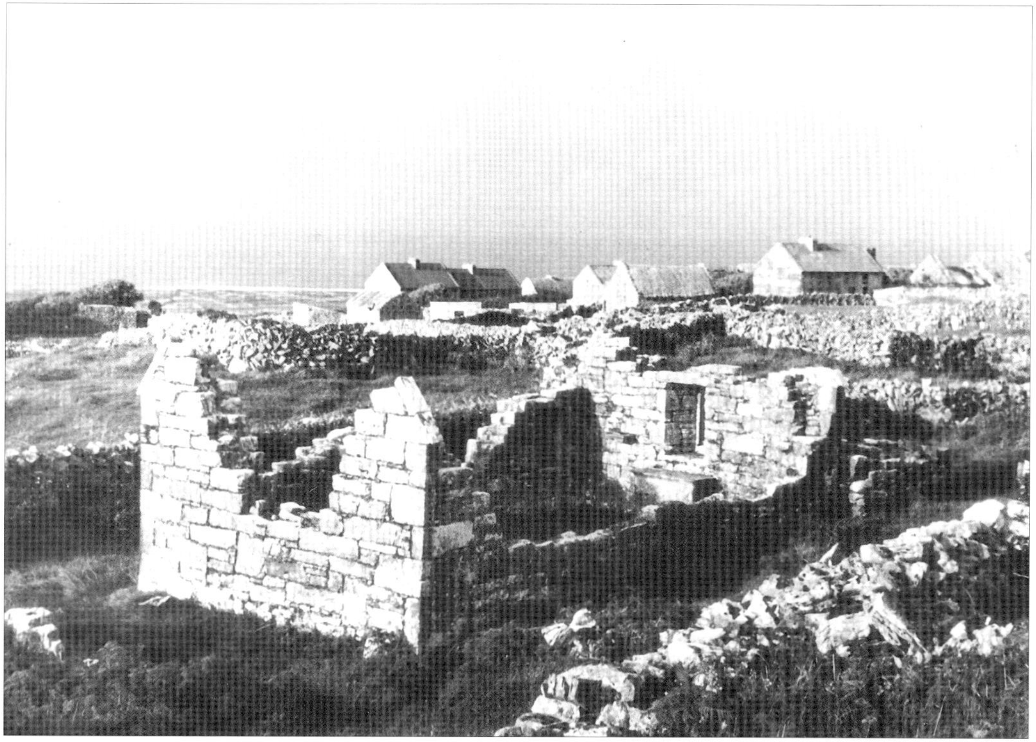

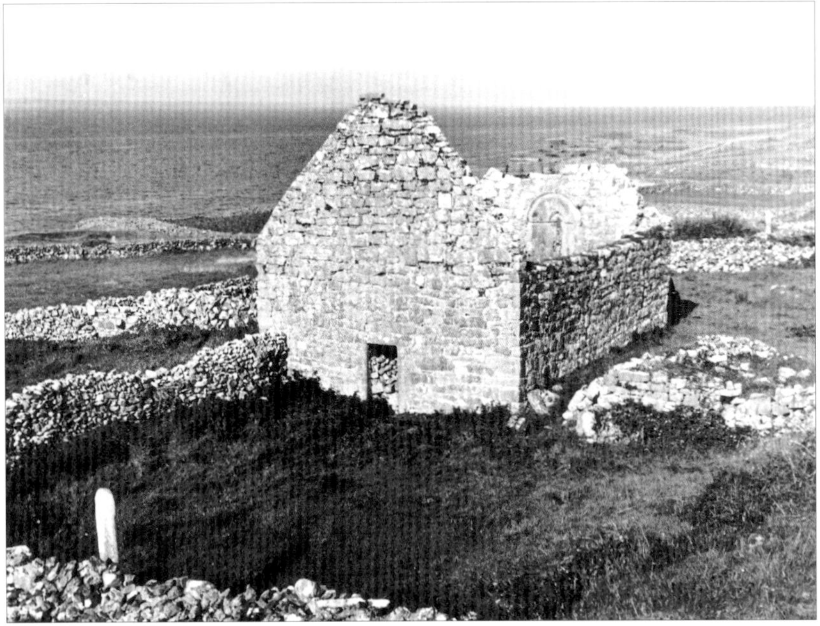

Left: Teampall Chiaráin at Mainstir, Inis Mór. Note the cross-slab in the enclosure. It will be seen in detail later. The Children's Graveyard is the small area left of centre.

Below, left: Teampall Mac Duagh, dedicated to the founding saint of Kilmacduagh, County Galway. The left half of this church was built with huge blocks of stone in the eleventh century. The half on the right, with its Romanesque window, was added in the thirteenth century.

Below, right: Cill Cheannannach, the Church of the Canons, stands near the shore at the eastern end of Inis Meáin. Note the projecting corbels which we have not seen hitherto. The interior shrubbery has now been removed.

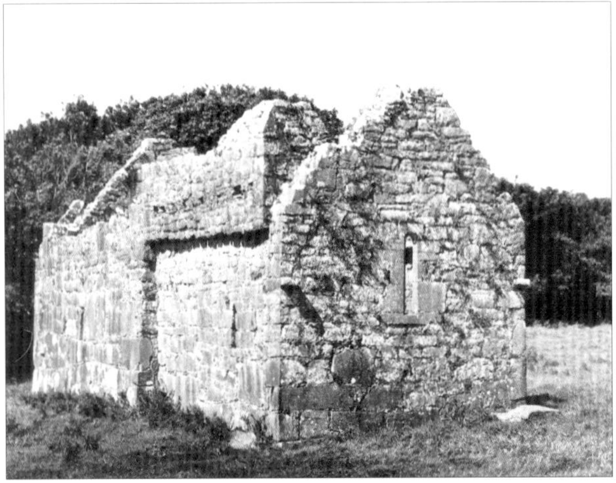

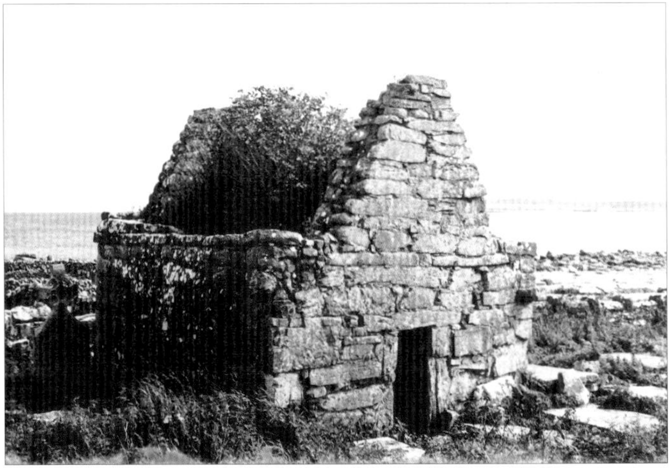

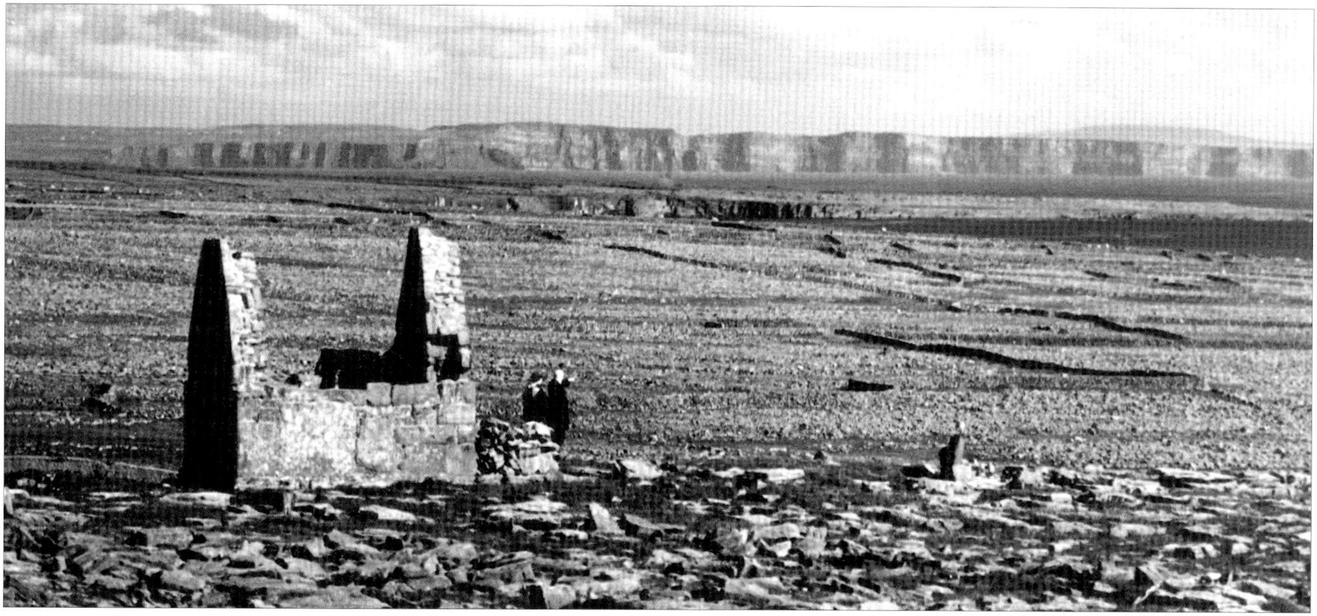

Teampall Bheanáin, with the coastline of Country Clare in the background. This is the oldest church on Aran and it is unique in being oriented towards the north. It stands on the skyline overlooking the airport of Inis Mór.
Below: Teampall Éinne stands in Teaglach Éinne, St. Enda's graveyard. The eighth century graveyard seen in the background is still in use.

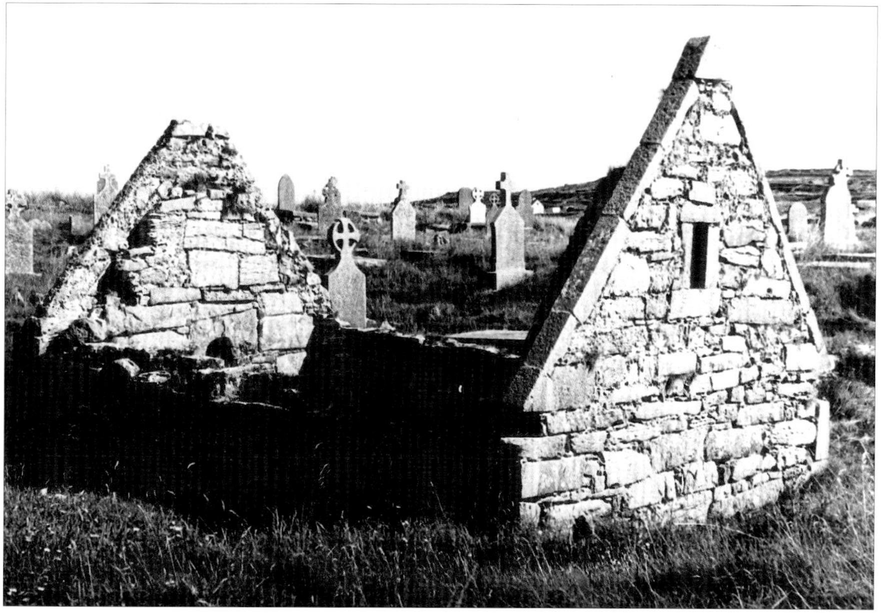

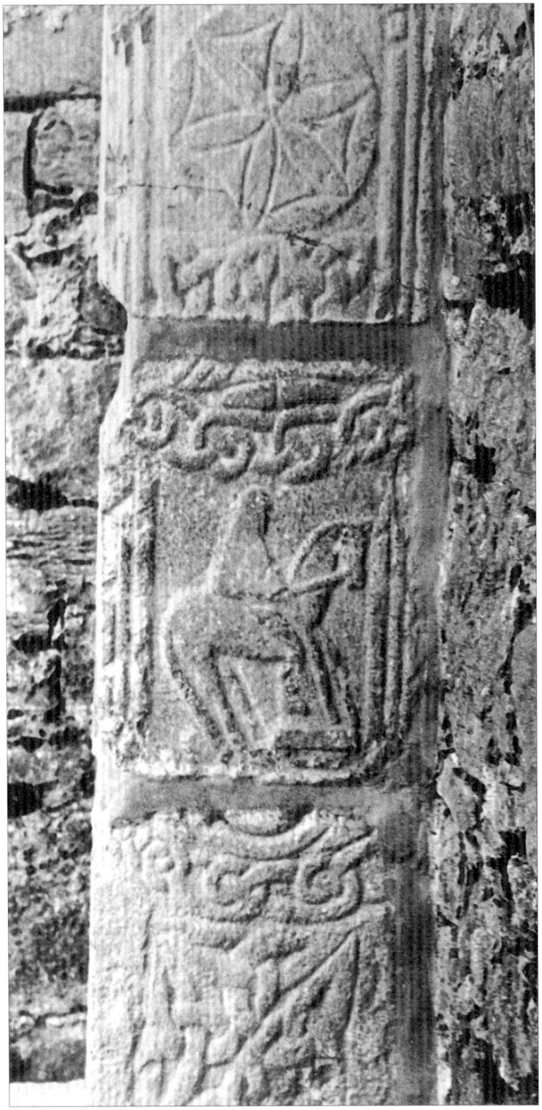

Fragments of the High Cross at Teaglach Éinne. Smashed in Cromwellian times, these are three of the five extant pieces. They have been cemented together, but probably not in the correct order. St Enda on his horse is believed to have been above the circular floral carving on the original High Cross.

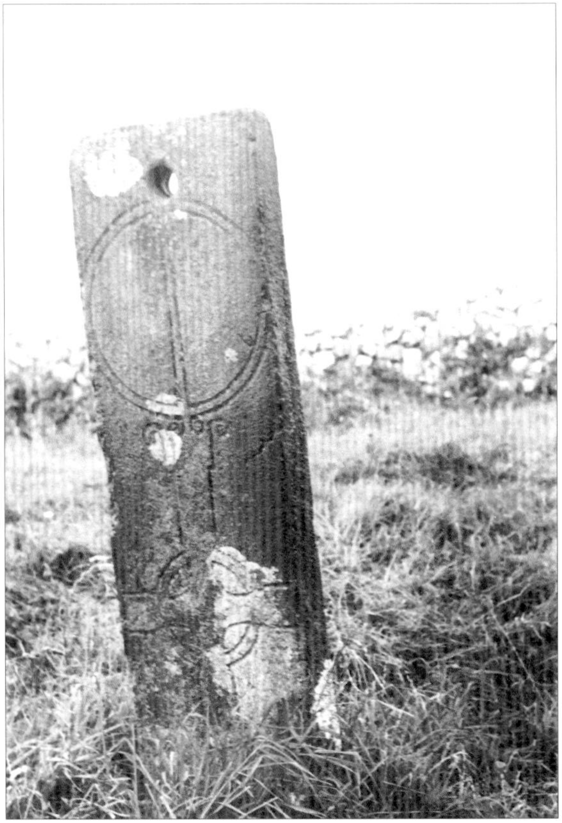

Above: Cross-slab with hole, beside Teampall Chiaráin. The hole originally held the gnomon of a sundial but in recent centuries it has been called "The Wishing Hole". A scarf or other article of clothing is passed through the hole while making a wish.

Facing, top left: Tom Hernon stands beside na Clocha Móra in the graveyard at Teampall on Ceathrar Álainn. Tradition tells us that this giant slab marks the grave of a saint but archaeologists think it may be a megalithic standing stone.

Facing, top right: Holy well near Teampall Éinne at Killeany. The two children are brother and sister, Delia and Michael Joyce.

Facing, below: Roadside cenotaphs near Cill Éinne. The central one has now vanished but the cross on the left-hand one has been restored. Dated between 1811 and 1876, the cenotaphs are reminders to pray for people like the McDonaghs and Millens. The photograph was taken in 1925.

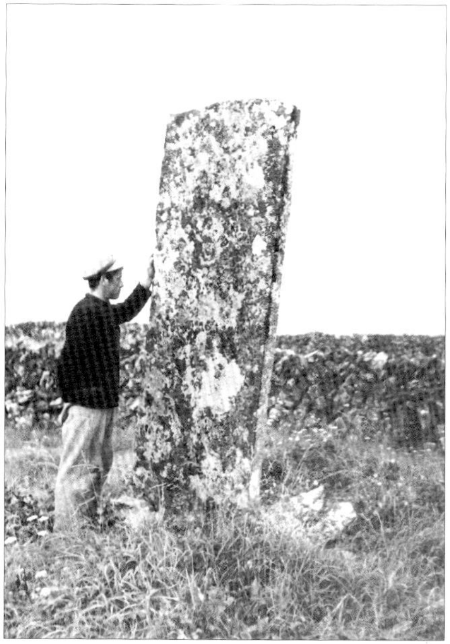

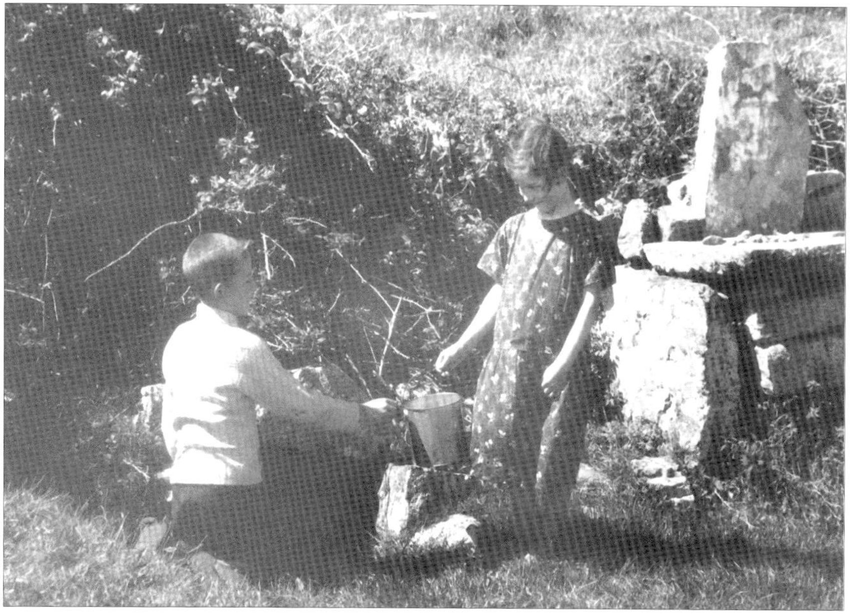

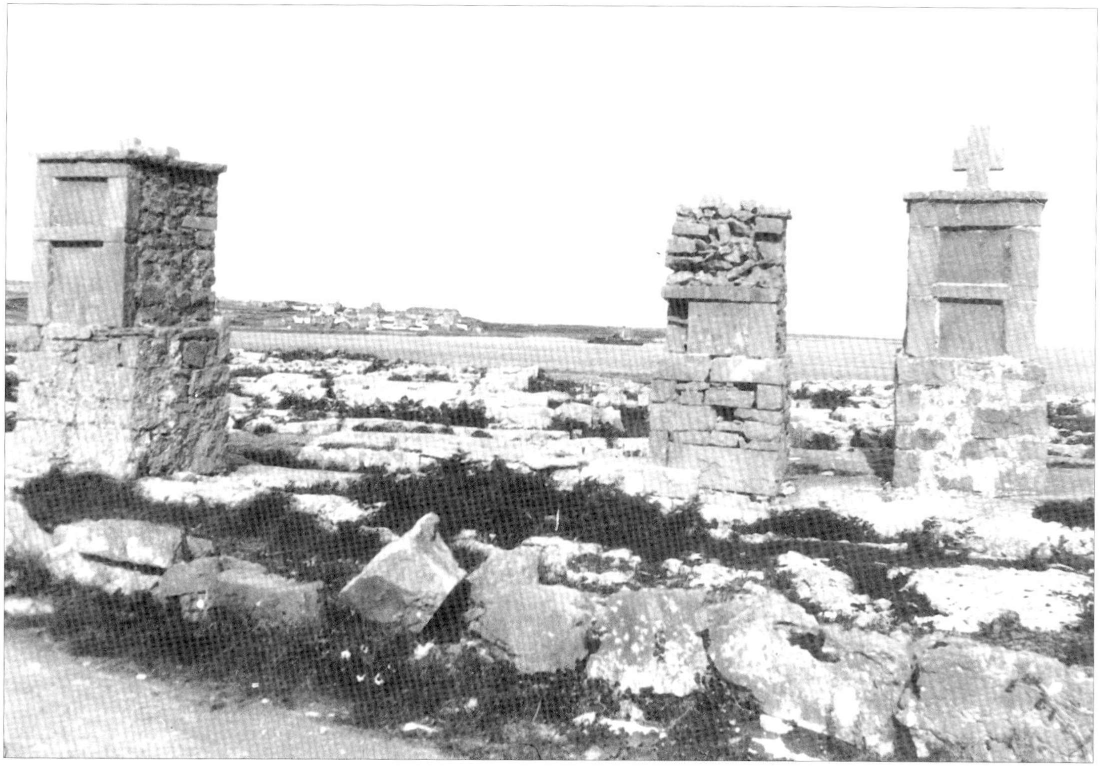

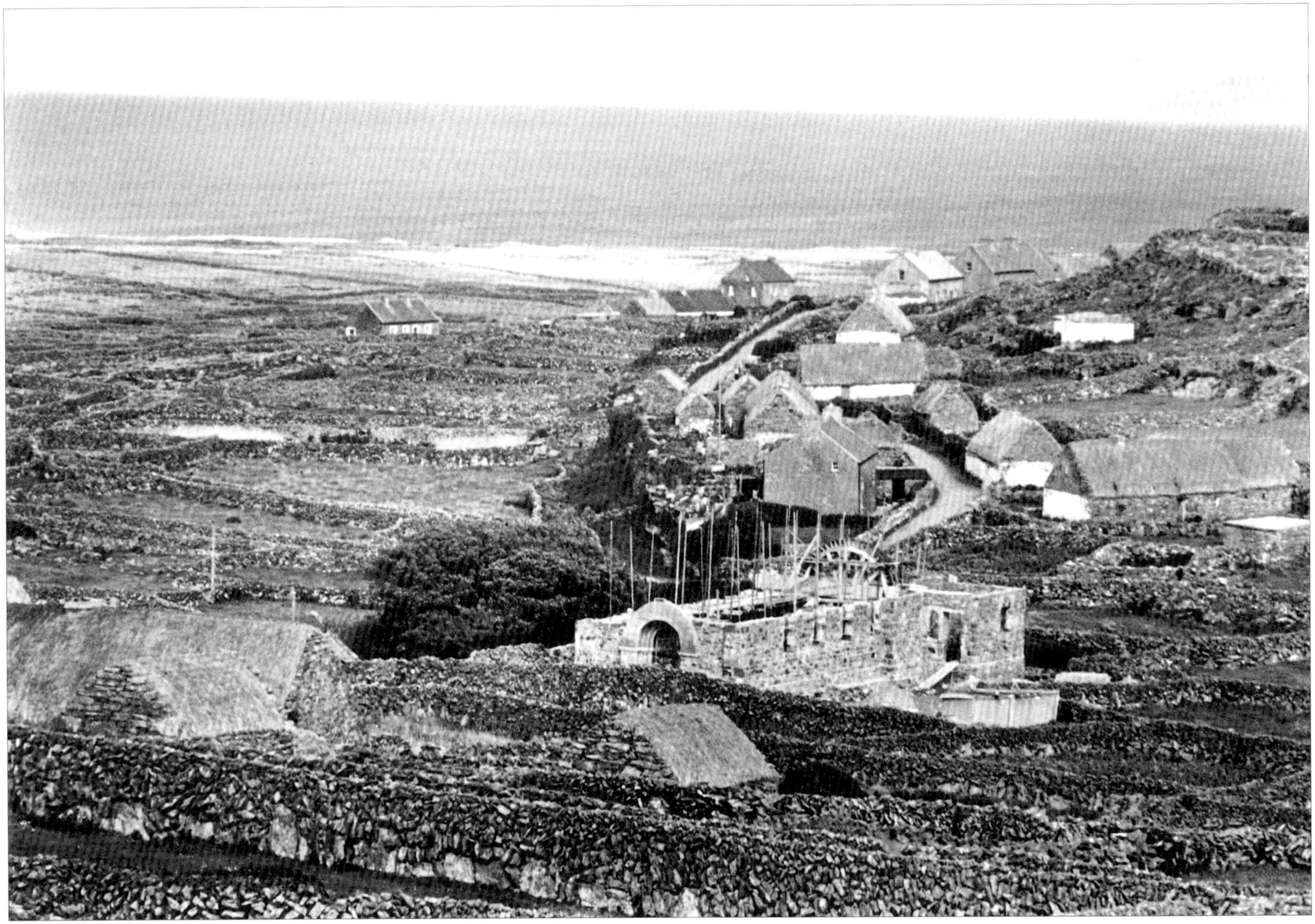

Churches are still being built on Aran. Here we see Teampall Mhuire, on Inis Meáin, in the course of construction. Behind it, the house with the tiny window in the gable end was known as 'The Priest's House'. Curtains hung in the windows as a sign that the priest was on the island. Synge's cottage, where the playwright stayed between 1898 and 1902, is just visible, centre left.

Chapter IV

Work

Apart from tourism, with its mixed blessings, fishing is still the mainstay of the Aran economy. In the chapter on boats and currachs we have seen the kinds of craft used by the trawlermen and offshore fishermen. People often fished from the cliffs, and they still do today, though often for sport rather than necessity. In Father Browne's day — when the economy was nearer to subsistence level — it was more work than play. Young boys were sent to fish for the dinner. Bream, at all times, and herring when they shoaled were readily caught from the cliffs and hauled up 200 or more feet on a homemade, double-barbed hook.

Cattle continue to thrive on all three islands. The Aran animals are healthy and strong-boned so they fetch good prices from mainland buyers. In Father Browne's day the owners took their cattle to mainland sales, principally in Galway. Nowadays the buyers come to the islanders.

The little man-made fields of Aran produce potatoes, onions, carrots, lettuce, cabbage, hay and rye. Flax was grown in the last century and when Father Browne came to Aran in 1925 there was still quite a few fields of oats — used both for porridge and animal fodder. The rye was mainly grown for thatching: in the photograph shown here we see it being turned to dry in the sun. In 1938 most of the Aran houses were thatched so the growing of rye-grass was important. Indeed a whole island, known as Straw Island, was dedicated to this purpose.

Up to the 1950s, most Aran clothes were made by local weavers from the wool of the island sheep. The women's skirts were made from *fleainín,* a heavy woollen tweed. Four or five yards of this cloth were used for each skirt. The material was traditionally dyed red, black or dark blue. The men wore a *bheist,* a sort of outer waistcoat made from undyed frieze lined with white flannel. Both the frieze and the flannel came from local looms like the one pictured in this chapter. Children, both boys and girls, wore hand-made clothes similar to their mothers' dresses. In 1938, the traditional women's shawls were used on all the islands; today they are mainly confined to Inis Meáin.

The building industry was a native Aran one in Father Browne's time. He photographed several houses in the course of construction. Whereas nowadays concrete blocks and imported bricks are generally used for building — with some exceptions, such as Gairm Scoil Éinne where the local limestone has been finely worked — the cottages of the past were all made of native materials. The introduction of cement made a considerable difference.

The thatched cottage, such as the one shown here, usually consisted of three rooms with the kitchen in the centre. The kitchen always had an open hearth and it also served as a living and dining room. Beside the hearth a door opened into the larger bedroom. Over the door there was access to a loft beneath the thatch. On the opposite side of the kitchen another door led into the smaller bedroom in which all the children slept. Since it had a low ceiling, there was space for a larger loft above it. Depending on the occupation of the owner, this loft could be used for anything from fishing gear to horses' harnesses.

The thatched roof of the cottages fitted flush with the gable ends, leaving no overhang where the wind could get a grip. Straw ropes were used to tie the thatch to the rafters for extra security. These straw ropes of various widths were also used for making beds, chairs and other furniture. The straw ropes on the roofs, however, decayed before the thatch and had to be replaced more frequently.

In the last century, seaweed was burned on many parts of Aran for the making of kelp. This labour-intensive industry has now been discontinued but seaweed is still used as fertiliser and *carrigín* moss is still collected by the seashore and exported as a delicacy. Women as well as men collected *carrigín* whereas traditionally, harvesting in the fields was considered a man's job.

Fishing from the cliffs could be work as well as sport. Here we see Michilín Dillane, the juvenile star of Robert Flaherty's film *Man of Aran,* fishing at Binn an Éisc. Note his Aran sweater, the only one seen in this book.

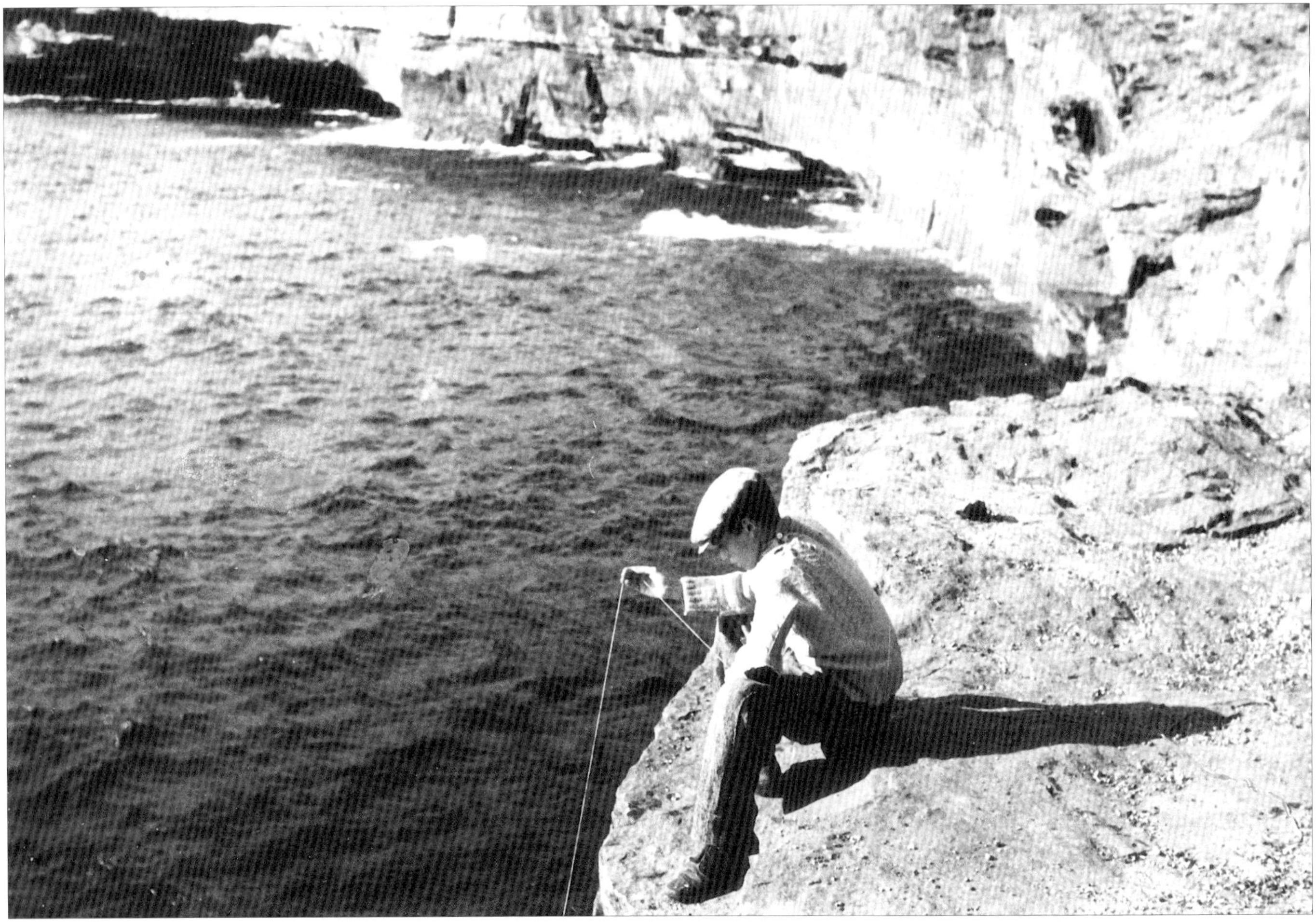

Stephen McDonagh disinfecting his trap before setting off to spray potatoes against blight. A knapsack sprayer would have been a recent innovation in 1938.

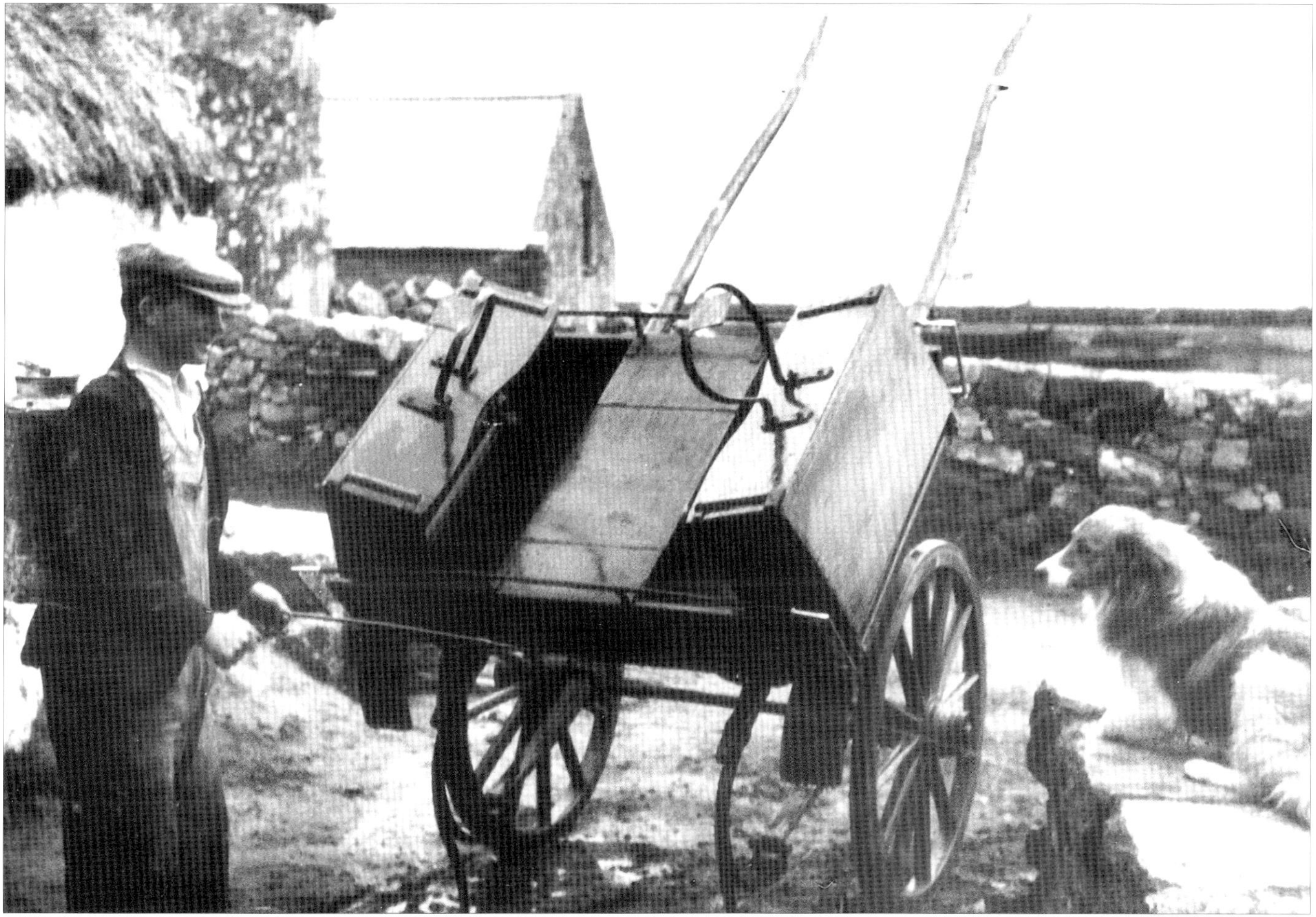

Harvesting at Kilmurvey, with Dún Aonghasa on the skyline. The men, and it was only men who did this work, are pulling up rye-grass by the roots for thatching.

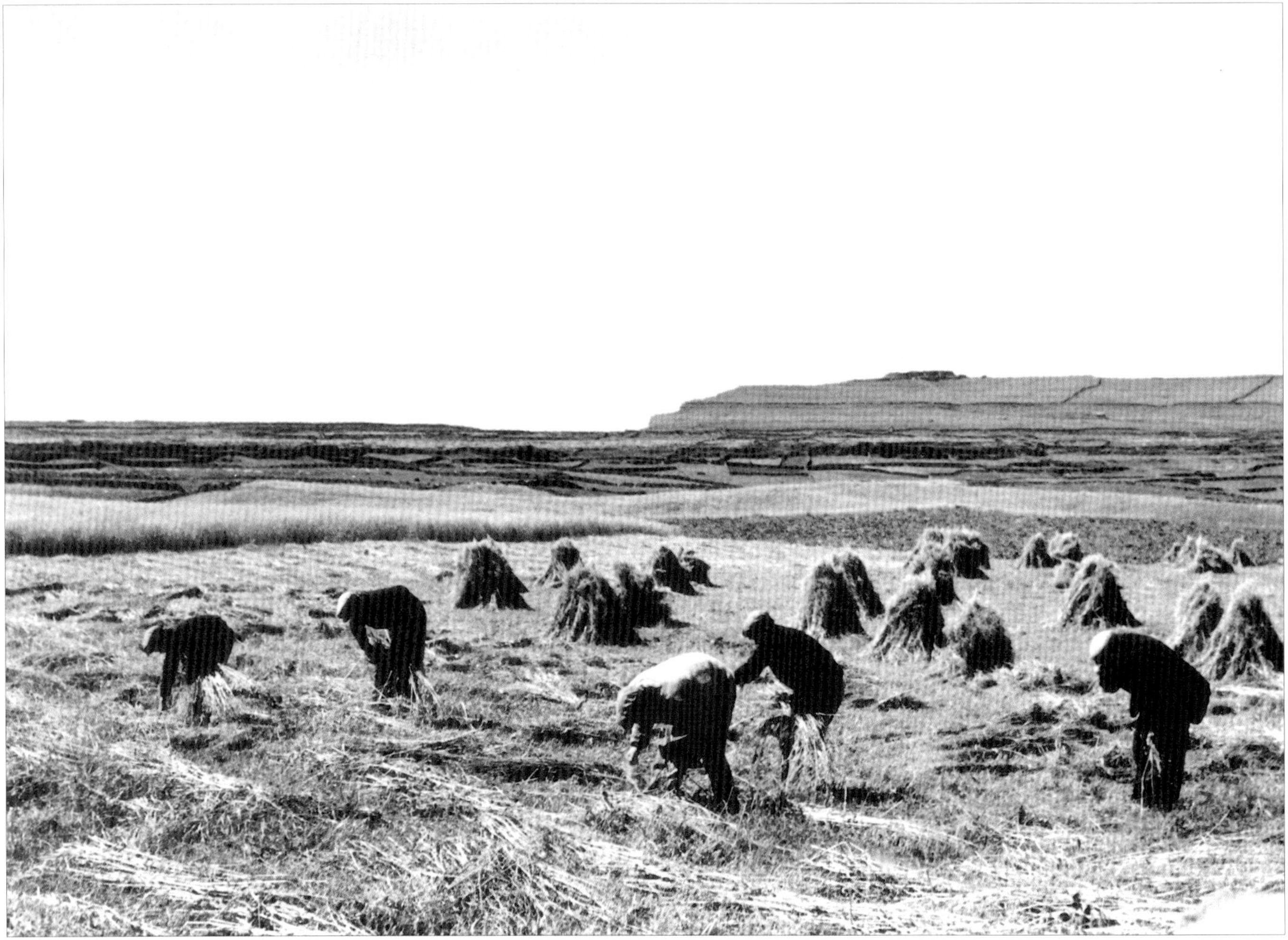

Monica Ó Congaile outside her father's thatched cottage at Kilronan. Notice how the rye thatch has been roped to the roof for security against gales. In the background stands the Church of Ireland. Its bell and slated roof are now missing.

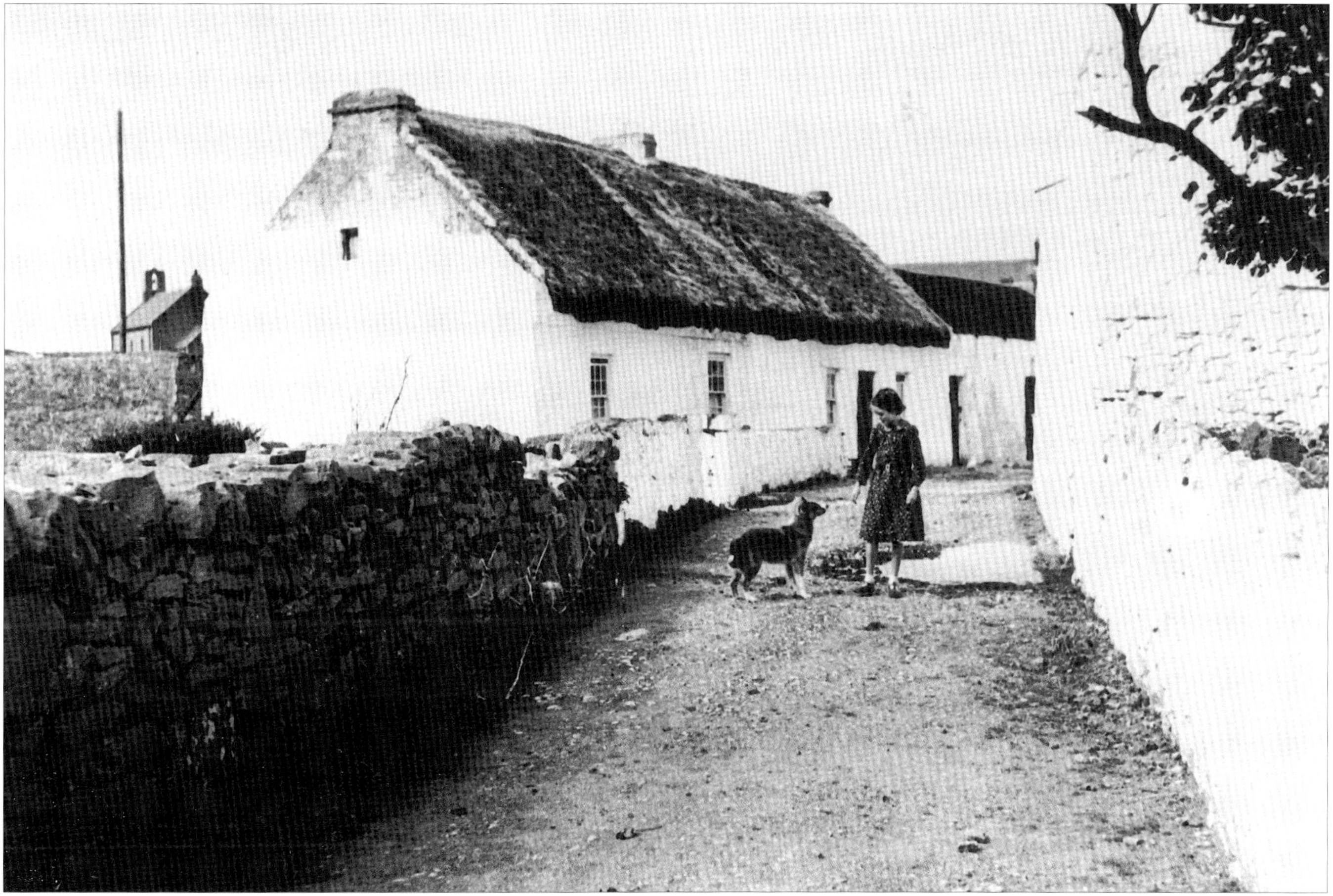

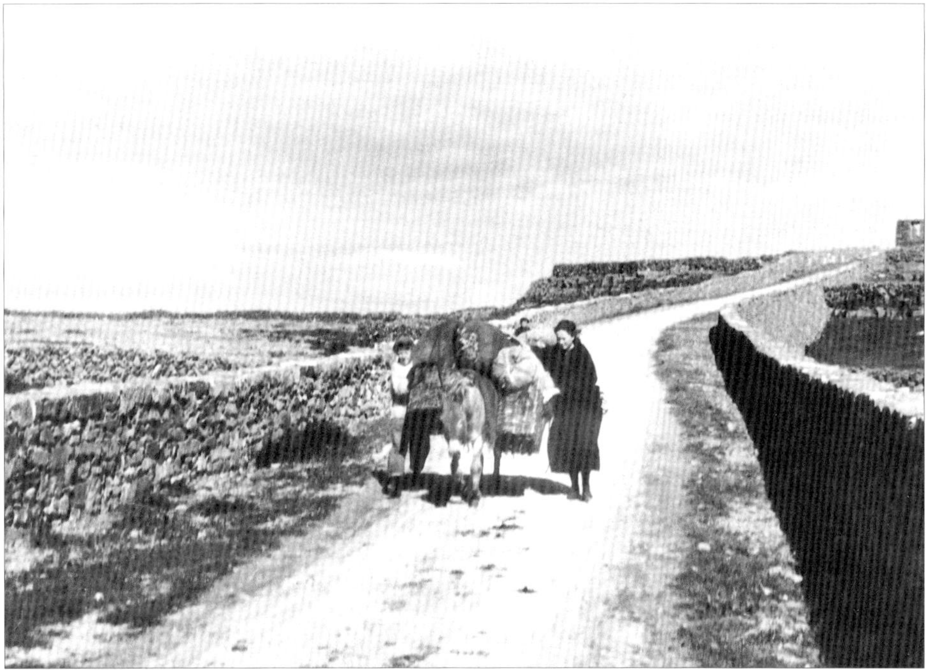

Girls bringing home their harvest of *carrigín* — an edible seaweed — to Kilmurvey. They are coming down Moloney's Hill. Schoolmaster Callaghan's house can be seen at the top right.

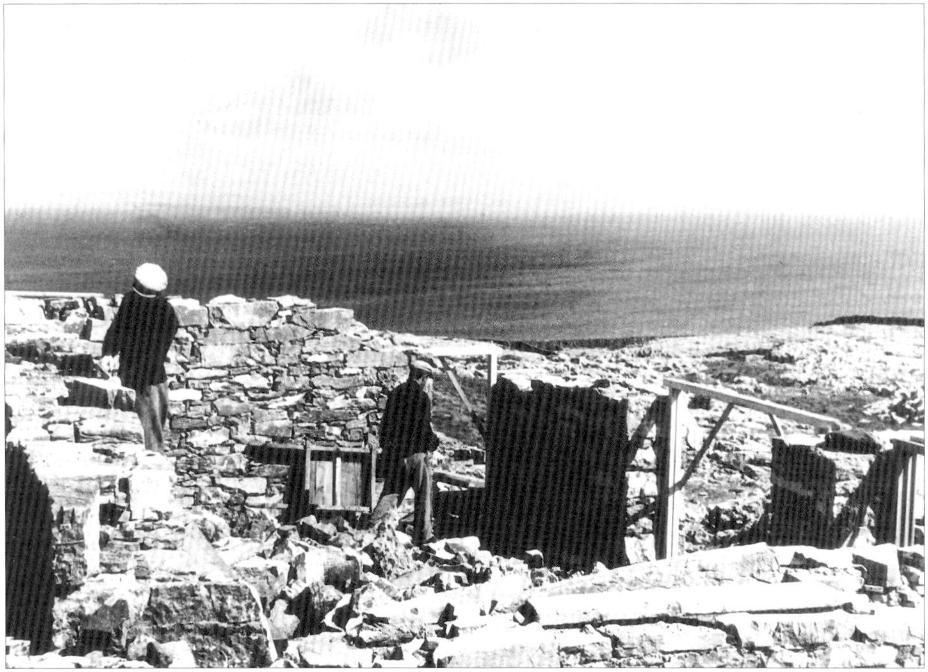

Building a cottage on Inis Oírr. Note the wooden hod and the wooden framework for door and windows. Many houses have been built on Inis Oírr since Father Browne took this photograph: it is the only Aran island whose population is rising.

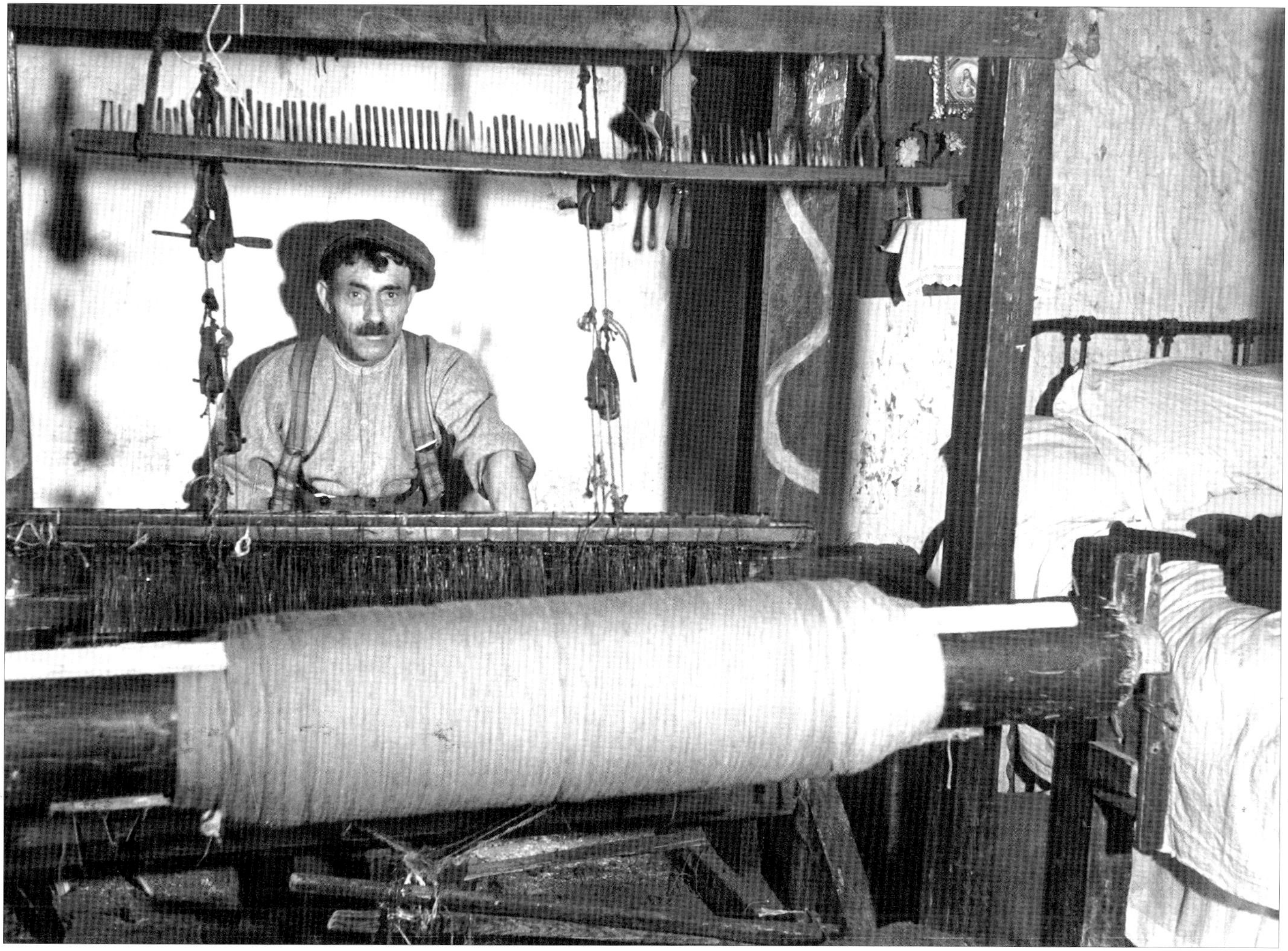

The weaver, Joseph Gillen, making *bainin* on his loom at his home in Onaght. Note his bed on the right and the picture of the Sacred Heart on the wall.

Overleaf: The stone-walled fields of Inis Meáin photographed from Dún Chonchúir. Hag's Head, County Clare, can be seen in the background.

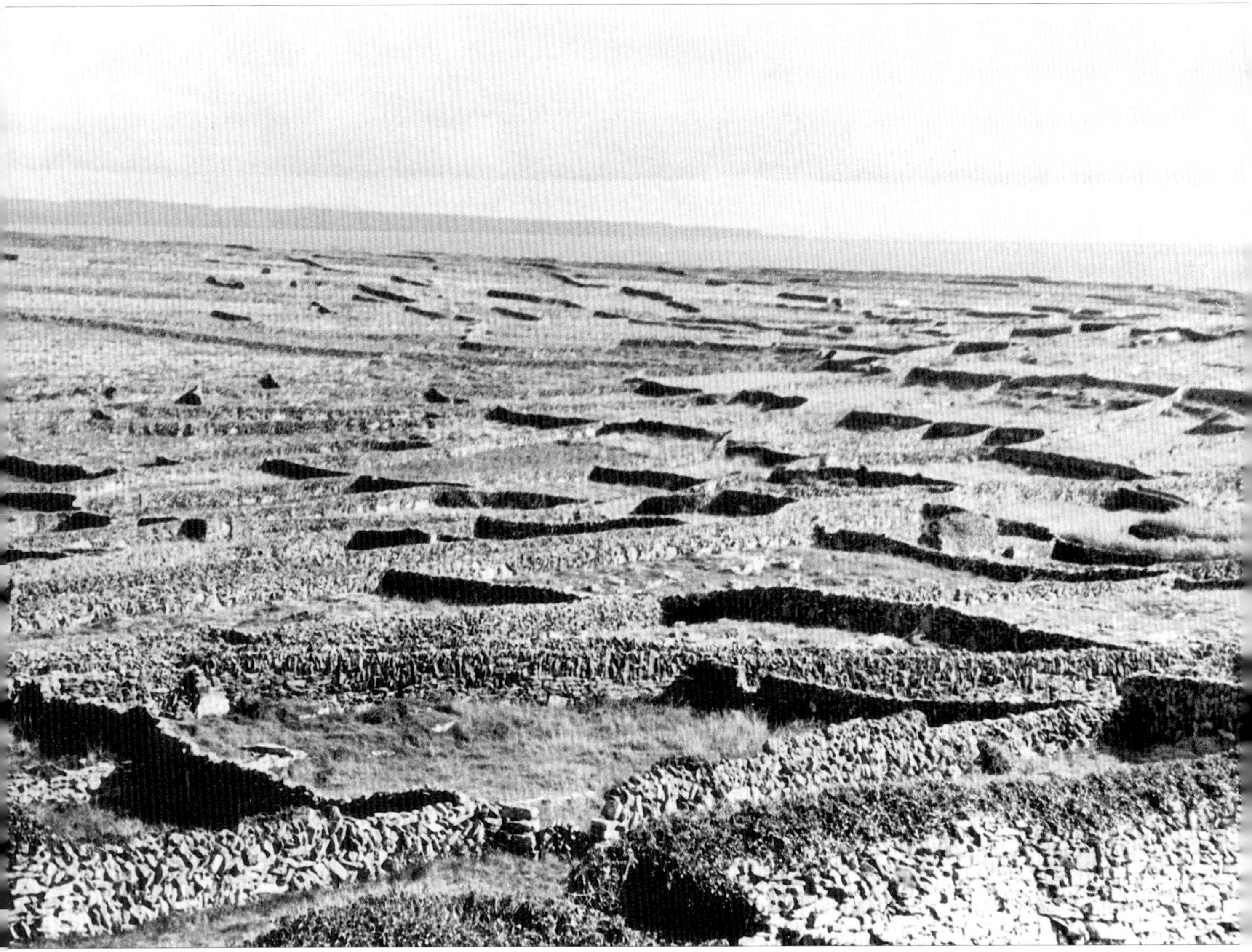

Chapter V

Landscape, Seascape

The Aran islands form a limestone reef at the mouth of Galway Bay. We have already seen that the landscape is dotted with more megalithic tombs, prehistoric forts and ancient churches than any other area of Ireland of this size. Aran is not unique in this respect, however. Orkney has even more archaeological remains from the same periods and they are in a better state of preservation. What is unique to Aran is the bare rock that covers the major part of its acreage, a sharp contrast to the fertile fields of Orkney. Over two-thirds of Aran's eighteen square miles are unreclaimable sheets of limestone.

Practically every field in Aran is man-made. Generations of islanders have carried creels of seaweed, sand, turf-mould and crushed rock to spread on the limestone base when the loose stones have been removed to build dividing walls. We see the same phenomenon in Clare and Connemara, but not surrounded by the frequently raging Atlantic Ocean. Furthermore, the fields of Aran are even smaller than those of the west of Ireland; it has been estimated that they have over 4,000 miles of stone walls.

The islands, in fact, are an extension of the Burren in the north of County Clare and were once part of that mainland. Inis Mór is eight miles long and two miles across at its widest, giving a total of 7,635 acres. Inis Meáin is three miles long and two miles wide, with 2,252 acres. Inis Oírr is practically circular, with a diameter of two miles and an area of 1,400 acres; six miles of ocean now separate it from the coast to which it was once joined. The islands lie about a mile and a half apart with the Foul Sound separating Inis Oírr from Inis Meáin (which was once called St Gregory's Isle) and Gregory's Sound separating the two larger islands.

The highest point on Inis Mór is 406 feet above sea level; the middle island reaches to 275 feet and the eastern one to 212 feet. Father Browne photographed the three islands from these vantage points and the patchwork quilt-like pattern of the stone-walled fields comes out clearly in his pictures. The bare rock flags used for house foundations are likewise captured in one of these photographs.

On its coastline, Inis Mór has the highest cliffs in Aran. On its west and south-west these awesome cliffs have an average height of 165 feet and are over 300 feet high near Dún Aonghasa. The vertical jointing of the limestone strata is responsible for the nature of the cliffs and explains why huge rockfalls occur in stormy weather such as it occurred in February 1997 when thousands of tons of enormous blocks of rock collapsed into the sea.

When the cliffs have been undercut by the waves, as seen in one of the photographs here, the fallen blocks of stone with their regular edges and cubic shape form an effective breakwater that helps prevent further erosion. However, given their exposed position with wild seas frequently whipped up by winds of force 11 on the Beaufort scale (i.e. 64-75 mph), coastal erosion still occurs. Geologists tell us that since the Ice Age ended about 10,000 years ago, Aran has been losing between .0075mm and .015mm of its land every year. Facetiously, they go on to say that, at this rate, the islands will have disappeared altogether in another seven million years!

There is one very noticeable feature of Aran today that did not exist when Father Browne last visited the islands in 1938. The farmers have built water cisterns in practically every field. These large stone troughs have sloping collecting-shelves made from stone slabs cemented together. These troughs have been a godsend for the farmers and their families because Aran frequently suffers from drought and it must have been a back-breaking job to water the livestock before the cisterns were built. It seems surprising, but Aran gets a lot less rain than the adjacent mainland. For example, the average rainfall at Kilronan over a thirty-year period was 1,128mm per annum. During the same period the average rainfall in Connemara was nearly 2,500mm each year. Moreover, Aran has no rivers and the porous nature of the limestone makes water-retention difficult. Some fine day, piped water will have to be brought from the mainland.

Facing Page: An Aran village, Gort na gCapall, with author Liam O'Flaherty's house in the centre of the group.

The natural phenomenon of Poll na bPéist on the western shore of Inis Mór.

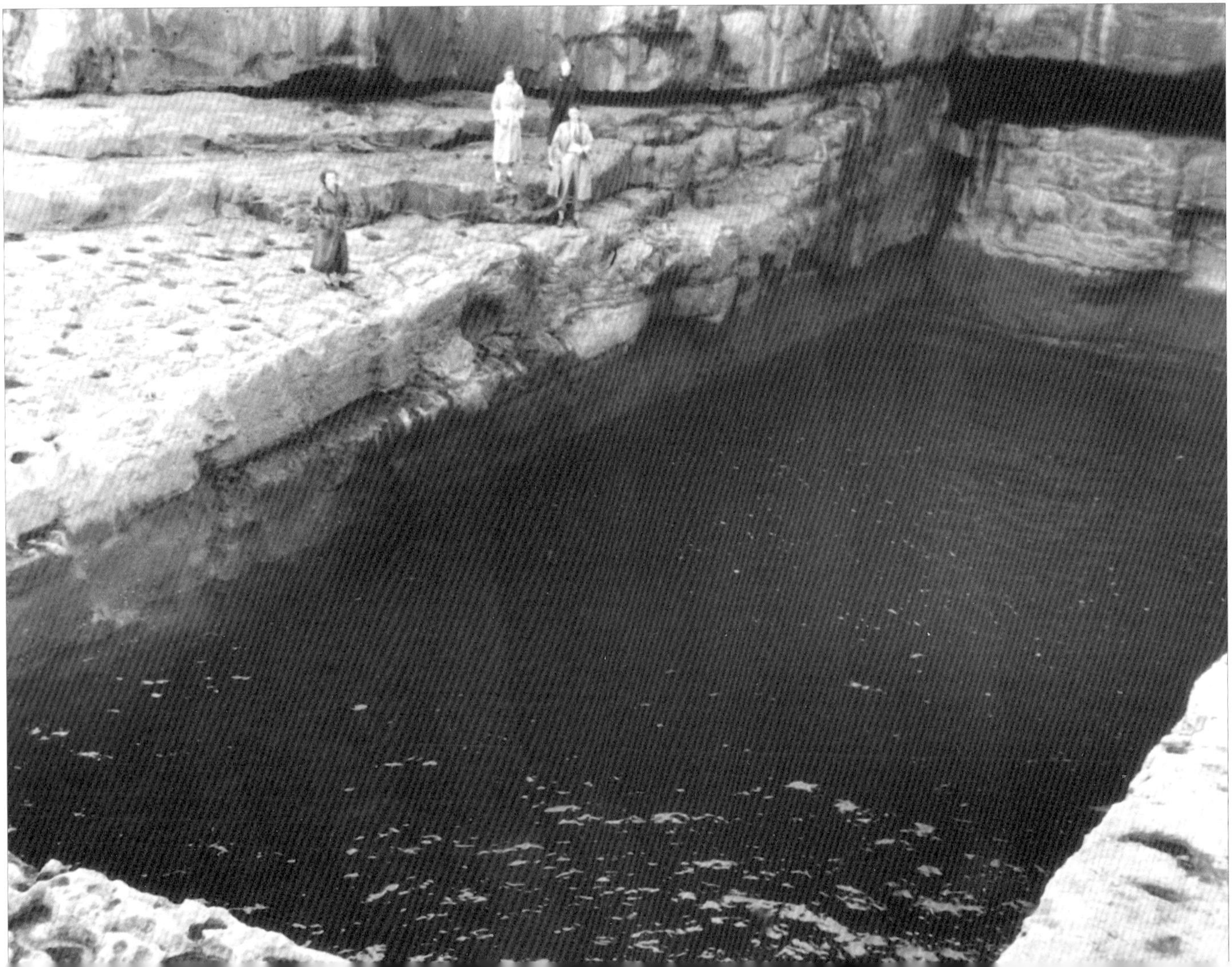

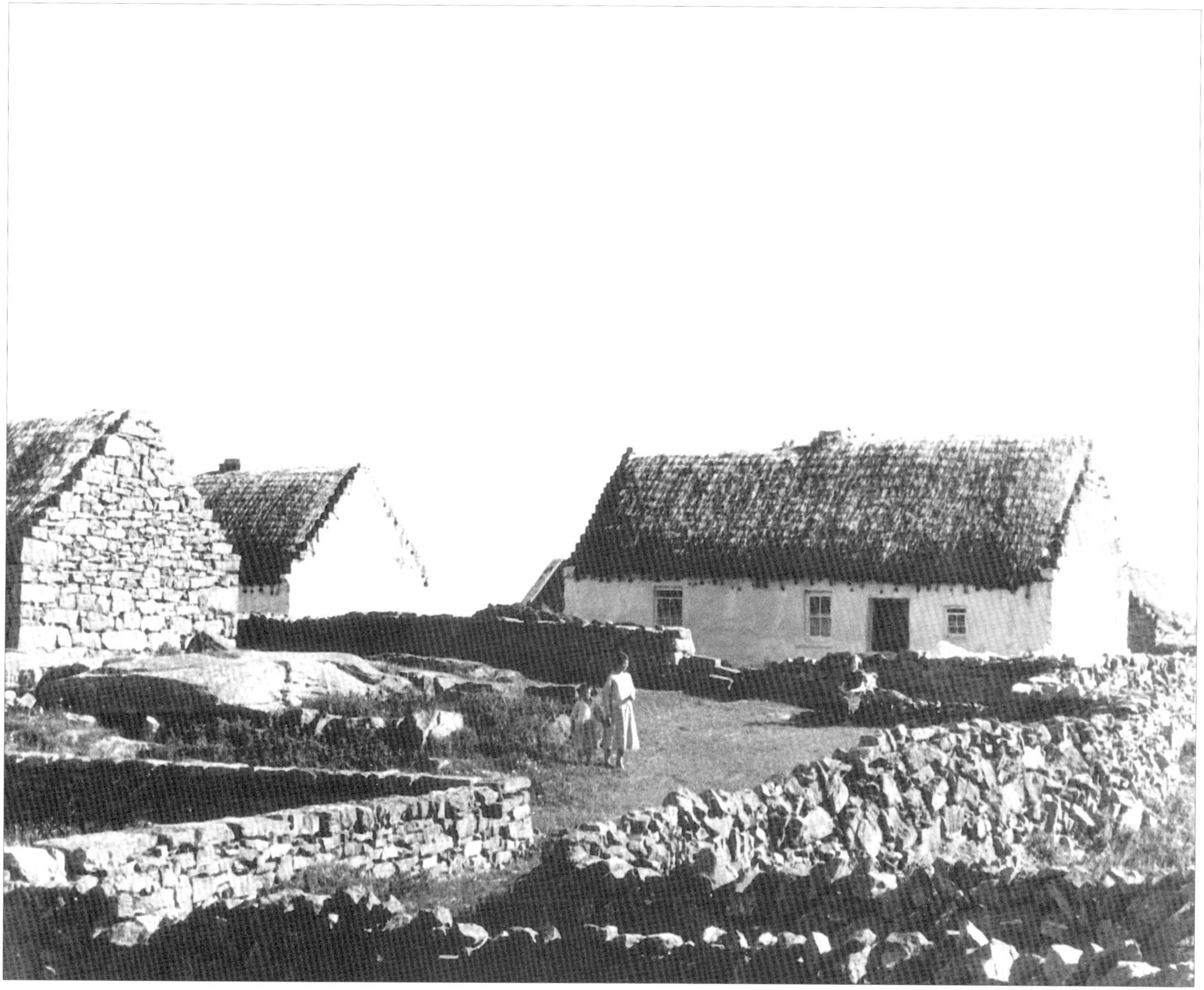

The limestone flags provide a firm foundation for Bartley Mullen's house on Inis Mór. It is still standing whereas the house on the left has been demolished. The cottages left of centre belong to John Mullane and John Gill.

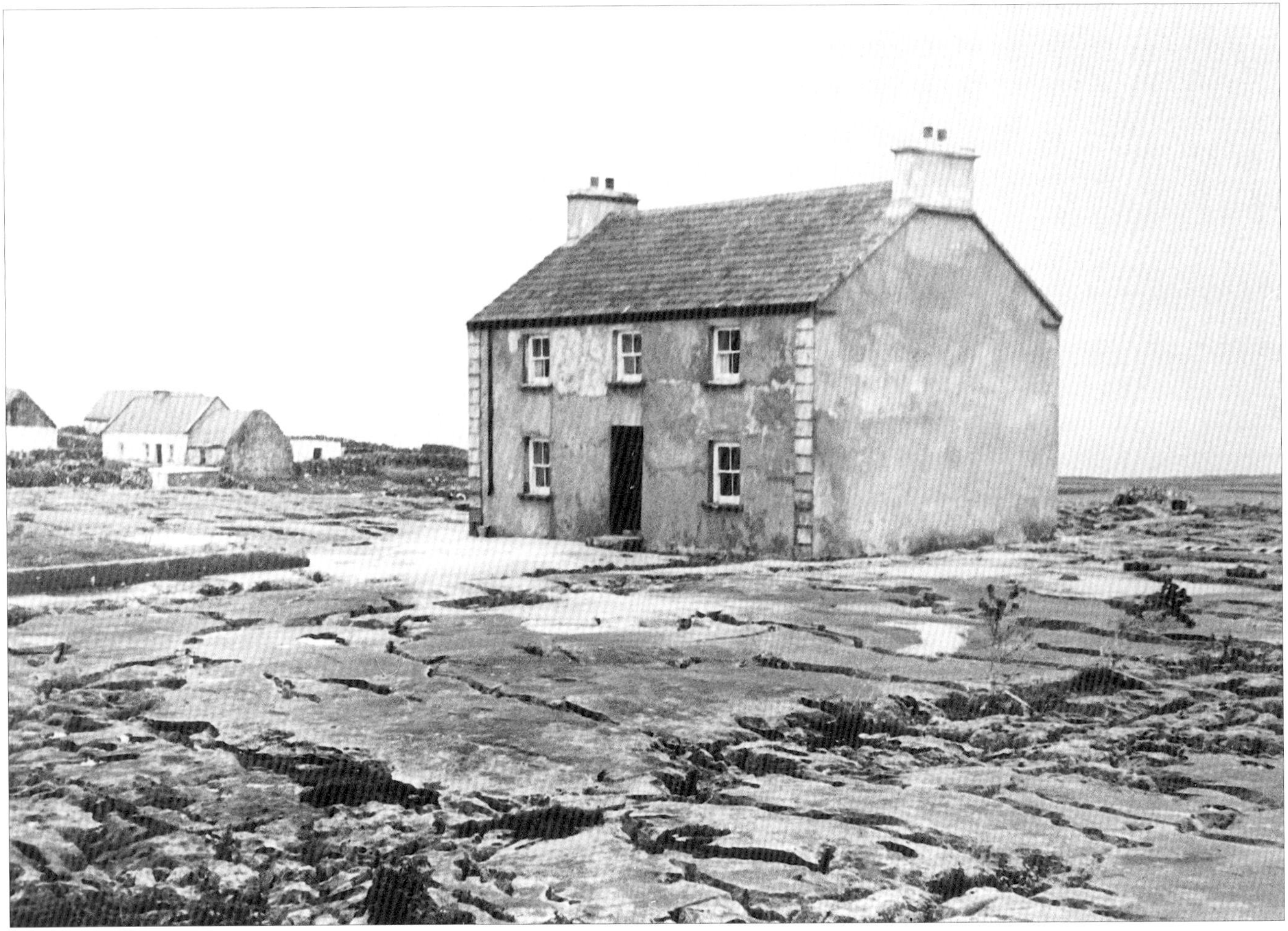

Girls on the clifftop near Dún Aonghasa. They are waving to the men in the currach 275 feet below.

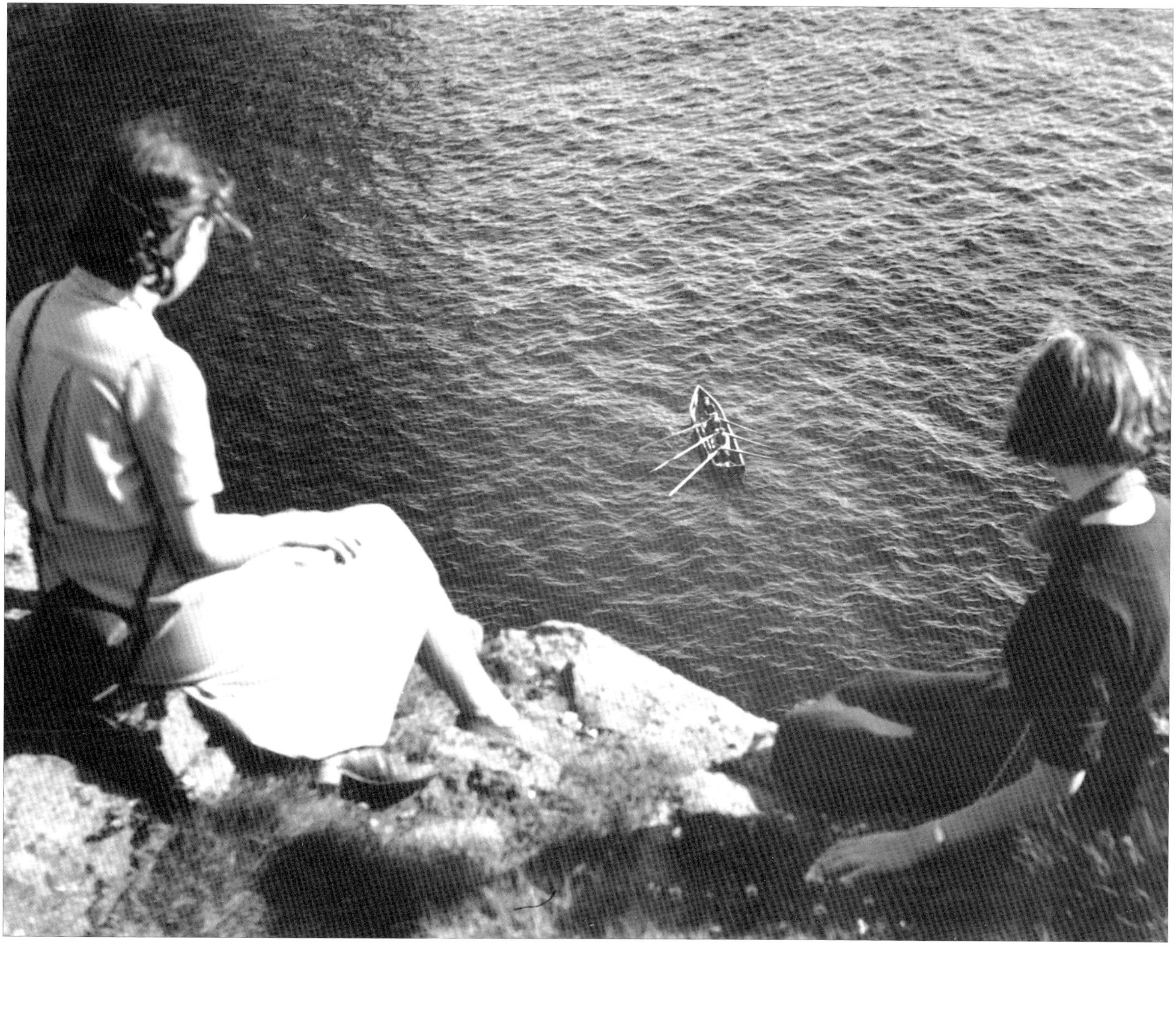

"Towards Tír na nÓg" (1925). The man is standing on the cliffs near An Poll Dubh. Tim Robinson's recent map of the Aran Islands marks Tír na nÓg with an arrow pointing westwards towards "the Land of the Ever Young".

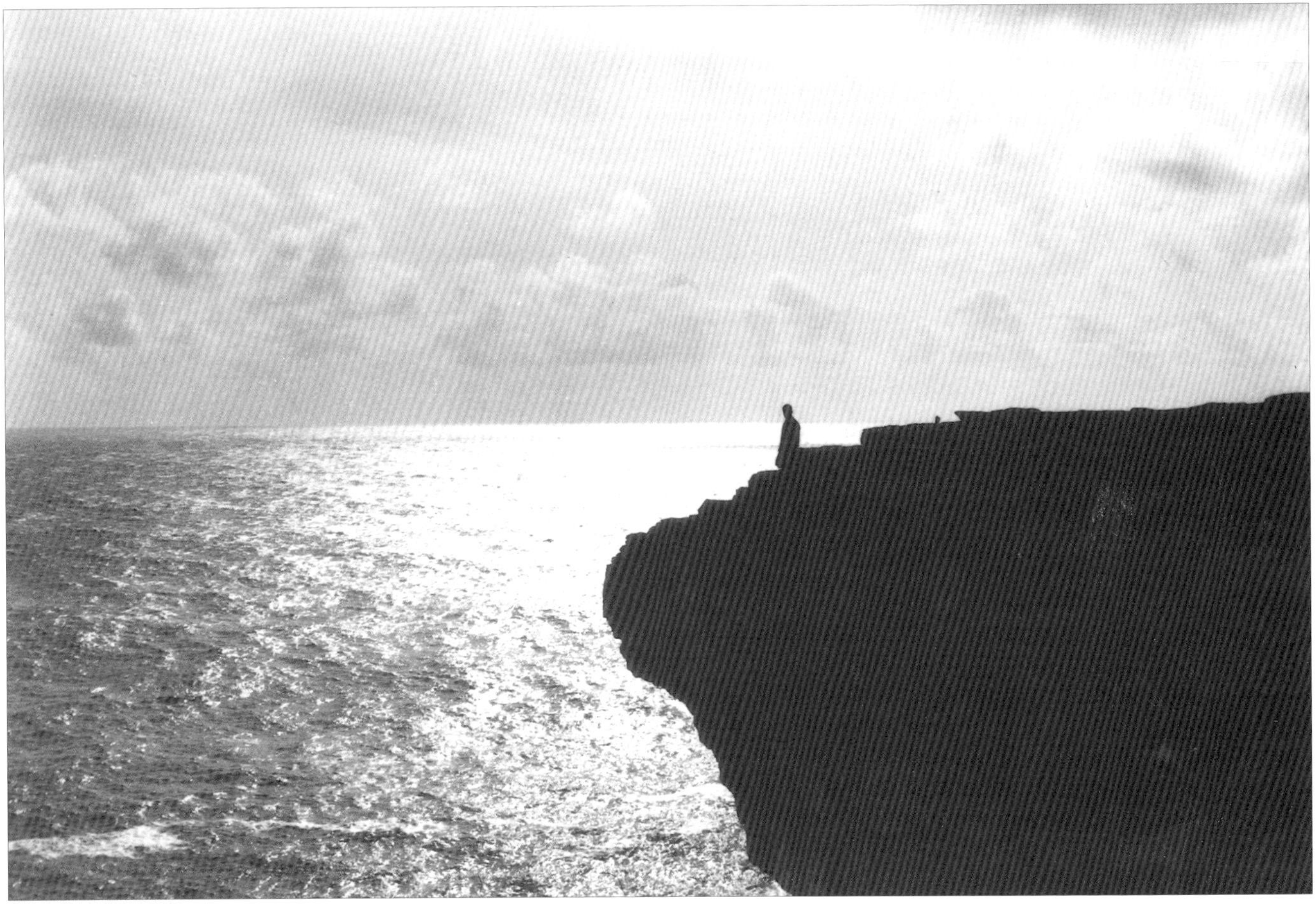

On the cliffs above Dabhach an tSnámha looking southwards towards the Cliffs of Moher, County Clare. Thousands of tons of rock collapsed into the sea here in February 1997.

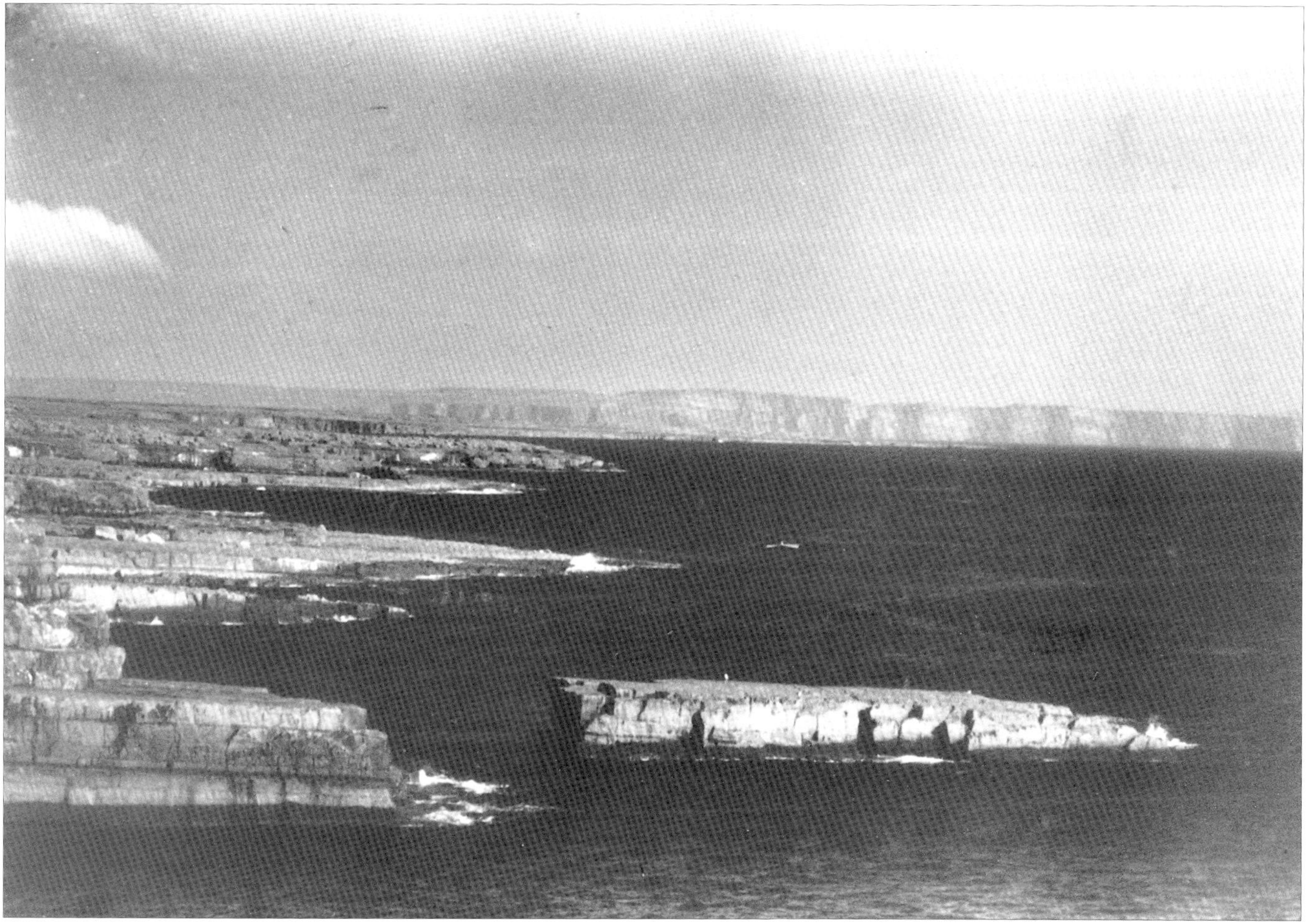

Sean Conneely with his son on Inis Meáin. Small boys on the Aran Islands were often dressed as girls for fear they might be snatched away by the fairies.

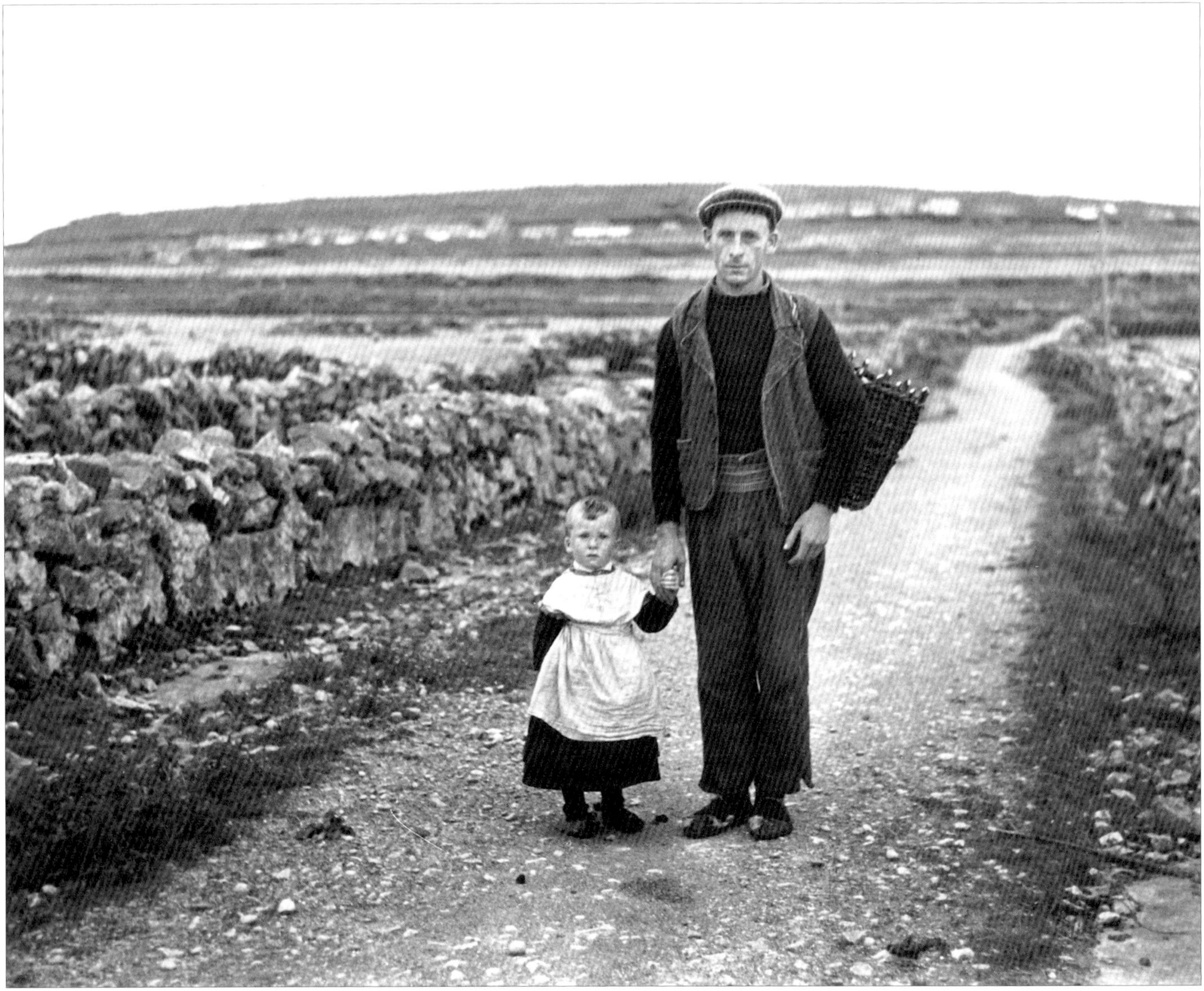

Chapter VI

People of Aran

In 1925, when Father Browne first visited the Aran Islands, the total population was 2,157 (1,368 on Inis Mór, 380 on Inis Meáin and 409 on Inis Oírr). By 1938 the total has dropped only slightly to 2,109 (the sub-totals being 1,289, 375 and 445 respectively). The latest figures (1996) show that there are now 836 people living on Inis Mór, 216 on Inis Meáin and 279 on Inis Oírr, giving a total figure of 1,313. Over the past twenty years, curiously, the population of Inis Oírr has actually increased by nearly 40 while the numbers on the two larger islands continue to drop.

One of the worrying statistics in Father Browne's day was that a disproportionate number of young women were emigrating from the islands. Mainly due to the booming tourist industry, this trend has now ceased. There are still a hundred more men than women living on Aran but the gap is narrowing. As is the case with some of other western islands — Inishbofin, for instance — there has actually been an increase in immigration. The relaxed island life-style has much to offer to people who cannot keep up with the urban rat race. The English lady who was a fellow passenger when I last visited Aran told me that she would never live anywhere else: she was coming "back home" from London.

In my experience, Aran islanders are a distinctive and delightful people. They are now perfectly bilingual, with the exception of a handful of elderly people on Inis Meáin who know only Irish. A point worth making is that I have found the people of Aran most considerate in not insisting on speaking Irish with me. Once they had noticed, early on, that my "school Irish" had grown rusty, they continued in English without making a fuss. In this they differ from the Irish enthusiasts of the mainland and from the natives of four other European countries whose languages I speak poorly.

The elderly islanders, in particular, have that dignity which comes from a life of hardship. They would be the first to agree that the young people don't know what real hardship is. In the 1920s and '30s, when Father Browne was in Aran, life was much harder and even the children he photographed looked different, maturer, than their counterparts on the mainland.

You will notice that there are no motor cars in Father Browne's photographs. Even in 1938 there were hardly any cars on the islands, and very few tractors. There were no island filling stations, so drivers had to import petrol and diesel in barrels. For maintenance or repairs, vehicles had to go to mainland garages. On Inis Mór today all this had changed utterly. Most families have cars. There is a bus service. And in the summer dozens of minibuses carry tourists from Kilronan to the prehistoric forts on the west of the island. And one can, of course, still go by pony and trap.

Another absentee in Father Browne's time was electricity. The Electricity Supply Board, Ireland's national supply service, reached Aran only in 1975. Up to that year there was no street lighting and only the wealthier families had their own generators. Domestic appliances mainlanders took for granted — hoovers, fridges, washing-machines and electric fires, to give but four examples — were unknown on Aran. The work done by women, especially, entailed far more drudgery than it does today.

The people have always had close links with Galway city where Irish was known by a majority of the people within living memory. In 1270 Galway became a walled city with strong trading links with Spain and France. To protect this trade, Galway paid twelve tuns of wine annually to the O'Briens of Thomond who were the Lords of Aran for some 450 years. In 1582 Queen Elizabeth I, despite Galway's support for the O'Briens, granted the islands to Murrogh O'Flaherty of Connemara. Although Aran has changed hands many times since then I have yet to meet an O'Brien on Aran, whereas I have spoken with dozens of people named O'Flaherty.

In 1652 the Cromwellian army captured and garrisoned the Islands. Many of the non-Irish surnames that still exist on Aran date from this period. In 1938 there were still fifty-five such names and Father Browne's friend, Michael Hernon, boasted that his was one of them.

With the Restoration of the English monarch in 1660, Charles II showed his gratitude to Richard Butler, Earl of Ormonde, by making him Earl of Aran in 1662. He was the first of a long line of absentee landlords. Dublin readers will be interested to know that he was the man who gave his name to Arran Quay, doubling the consonant just as Arthur Chichester doubled the 'l' of Donegall in Belfast.

In 1861 there were ninety-five Protestants living on Inis Mór, with their own church and vicar. When Father Browne arrived in 1925 this number had dropped to two. In 1938 the Protestant church appears in one of the photographs with a slated roof and bell. Today both roof and bell are gone. The ruin remains as a reminder that "this too will pass".

In 1896 William Butler Yeats first visited Aran. He was enraptured by the people and one can easily imagine him thinking of one of Father Browne's Inis Meáin girls when he wrote:

> Had I the heavens' embroidered cloths
> Enwrought with golden and silver light,
> The blue and the dim and the dark cloths
> Of night and light and the half-light,
> I would spread the cloths under your feet:
> But I, being poor, have only my dreams ...

It was Yeats who sent John Millington Synge to Aran in 1898 and Synge was so taken by the people and their islands that he returned in each of the four following years. It was he who made the place world famous with *The Aran Islands,* published in 1907, and his plays, *Riders to the Sea* and *The Playboy of the Western World.*

Since then, numerous writers of prose and poetry, in Irish as well as English, have continued to find inspiration in the magic of Aran. I must single out one of them, the internationally renowned short story writer and novelist, Liam O'Flaherty, a native of Gort na gCapall, many of whose books - such as the novels *Skerrett* and *The Black Soul* which are set on Aran - have been re-published in recent times by Wolfhound Press. Other Aran writers of substantial reputation include Mairtín O'Direáin and Breandán Ó hEithir. Indeed, the Aran Islands can boast altogether of sixty-three published writers, no paltry achievement for the people of Liam O'Flaherty's 'windswept rock'.

Man of Aran — 'Old Tom' Conneely of Cowragh.

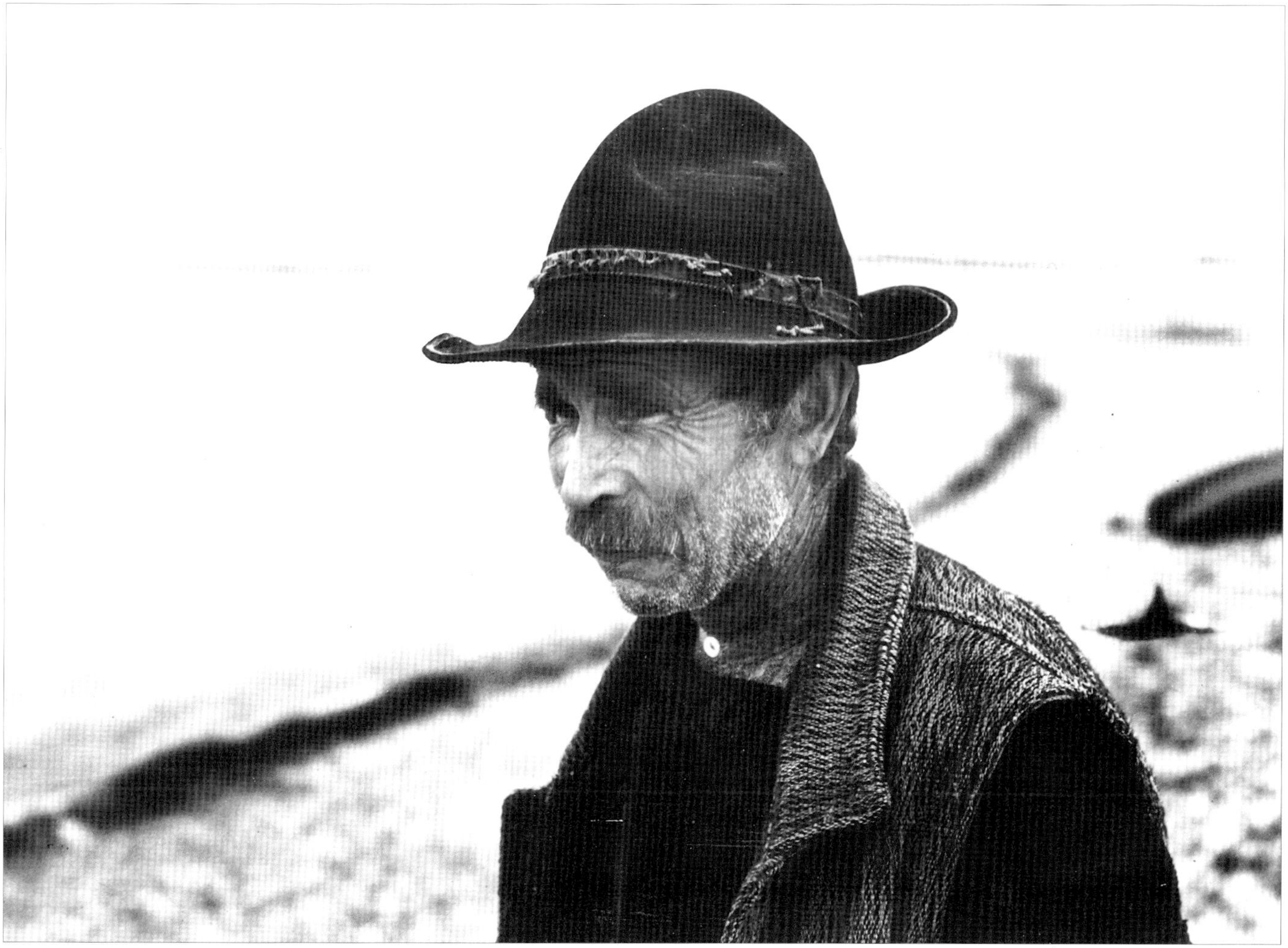

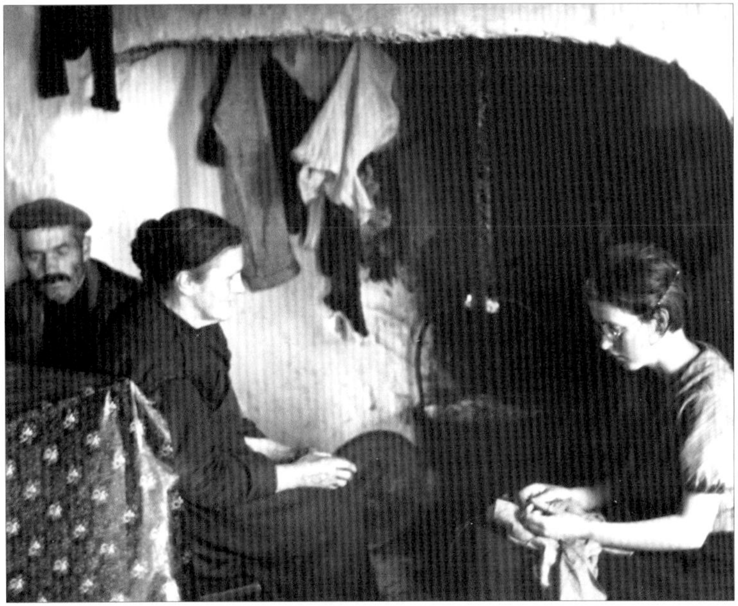

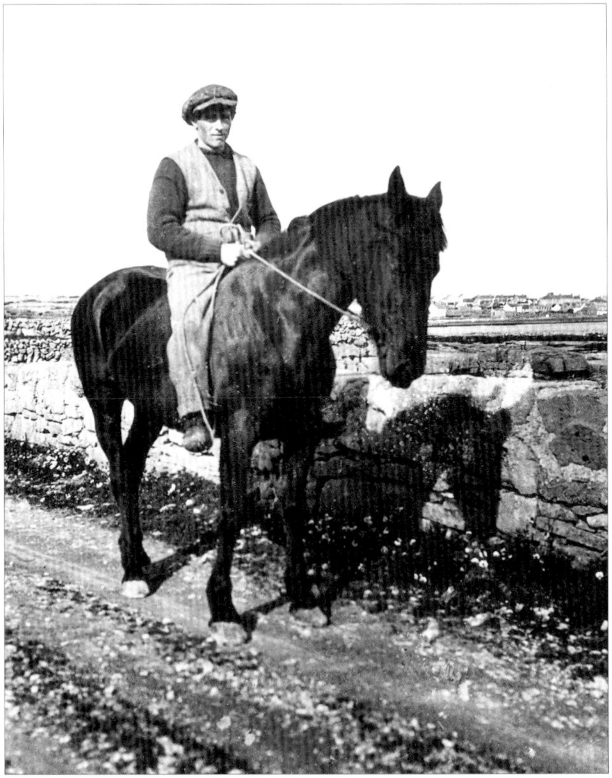

Above right: Sean Faherty of Oughill on horseback near Kilronan. Note his rawhide shoes. In Irish these are called 'bróga úléir' or bróga úrleathair'. In English they are given the exotic name 'pampooties'.

Above left: The Flaherty's of Oughill. From the left, we see John, his sister Annie and daughter Mary.

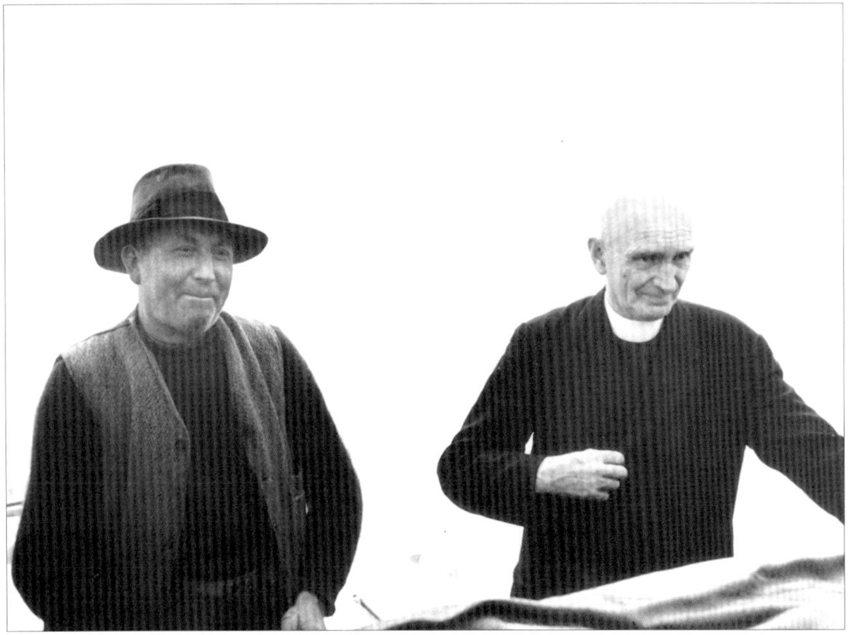

Left: John Gill of Kilronan photographed with Father John Keane S.J.

Outside the Post Office at Kilronan. The people are gathered here to listen to the postman — standing in front of the tourist with hat — calling out the addresses from the envelopes. He had fewer deliveries to make if letters were collected here.

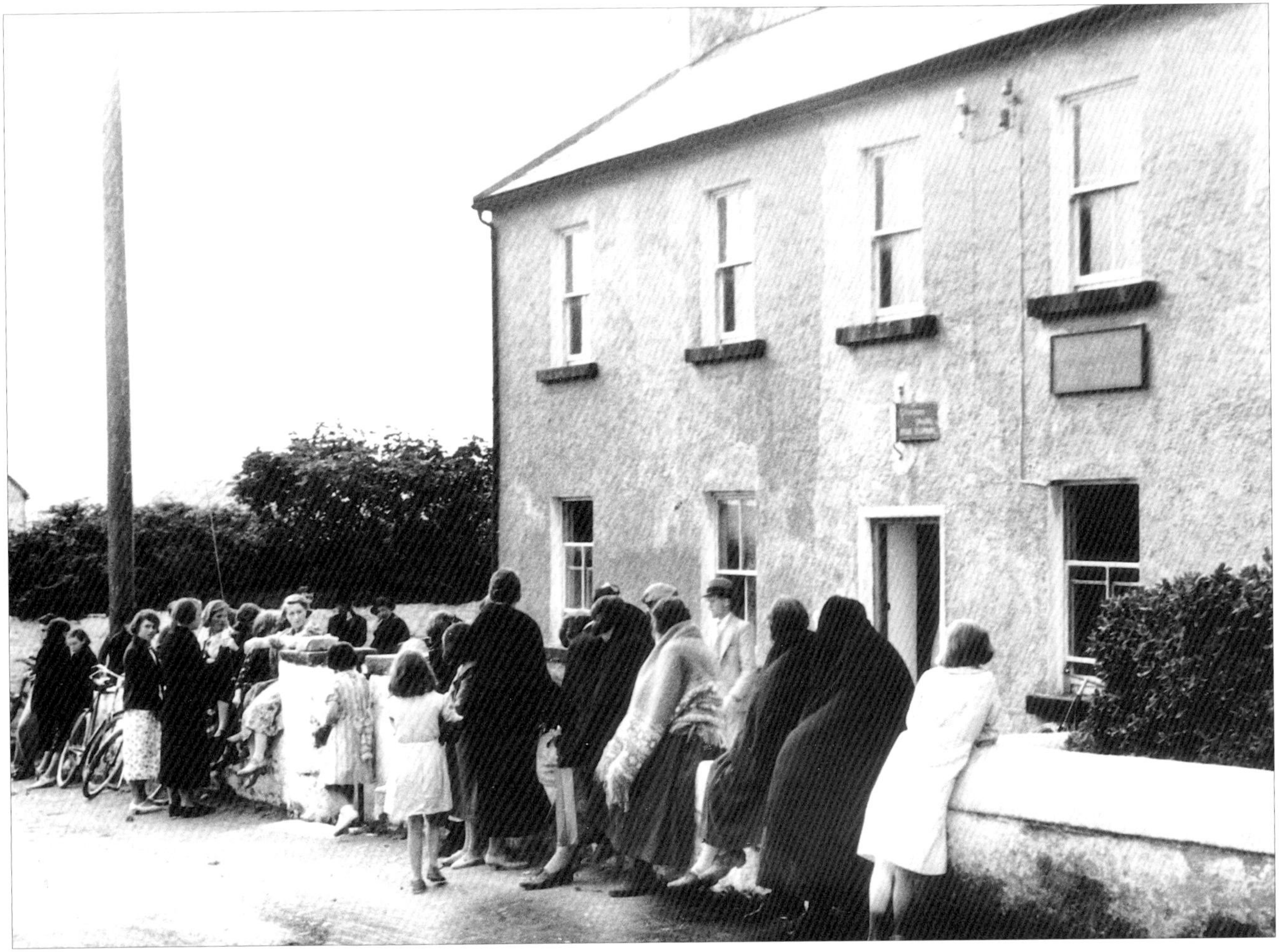

Father John Keane S.J. has something interesting to read to Tom Mulkerrin, Tomásín Faherty and Colm Mór Faherty.
The latter two were not related.

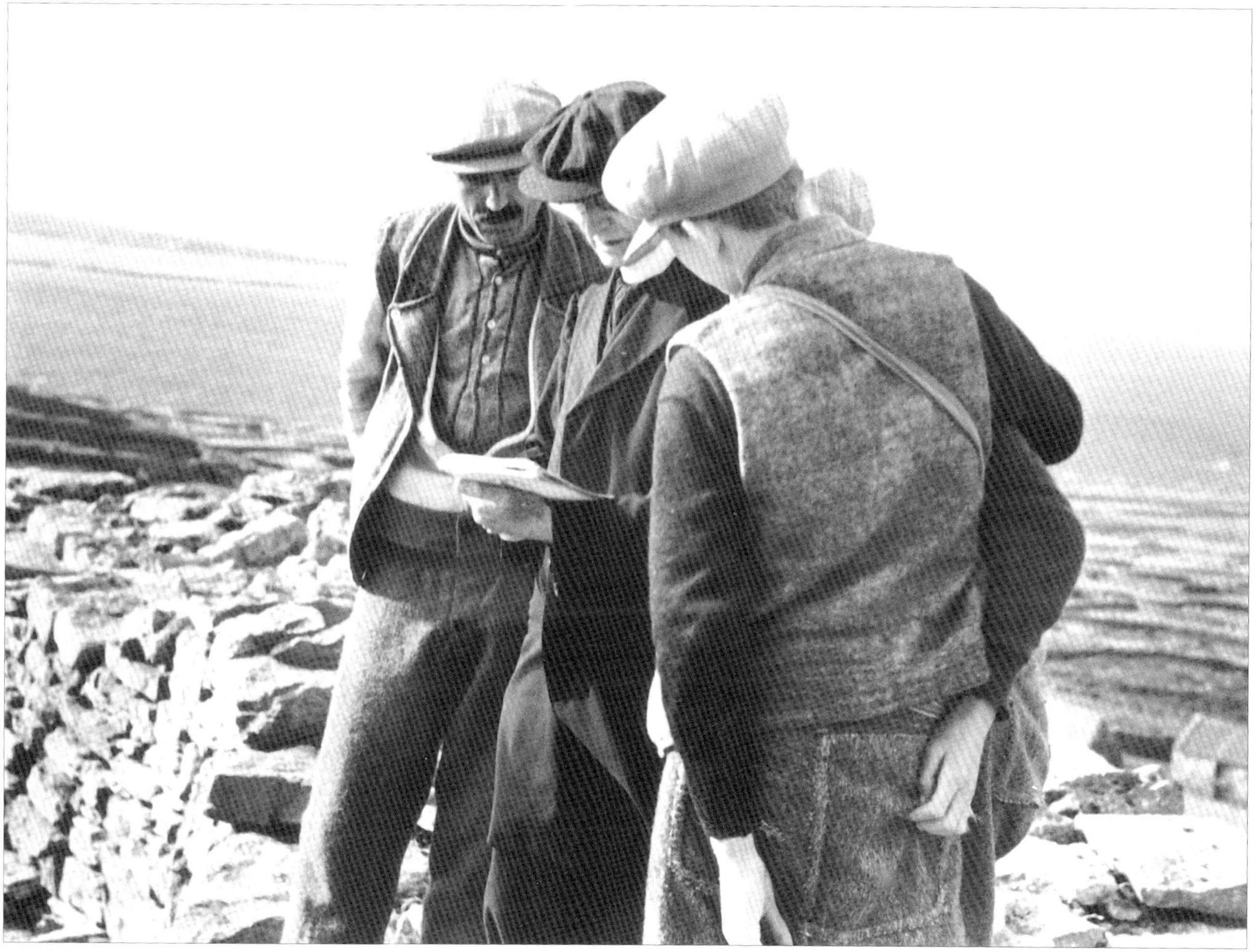

A happy group on Inis Meáin. From the left, the grown-ups are Nora Peigín Faherty, Mary Flaherty, Patch Faherty, Colm Michael Flaherty (at rear) and Margaret Folan. The children in front are Maureen Faherty, Colmín Michael Flaherty, Sally Conneely, Bríd Maher, Tomás Conneely, Ann Flaherty and little Maureen Flaherty.

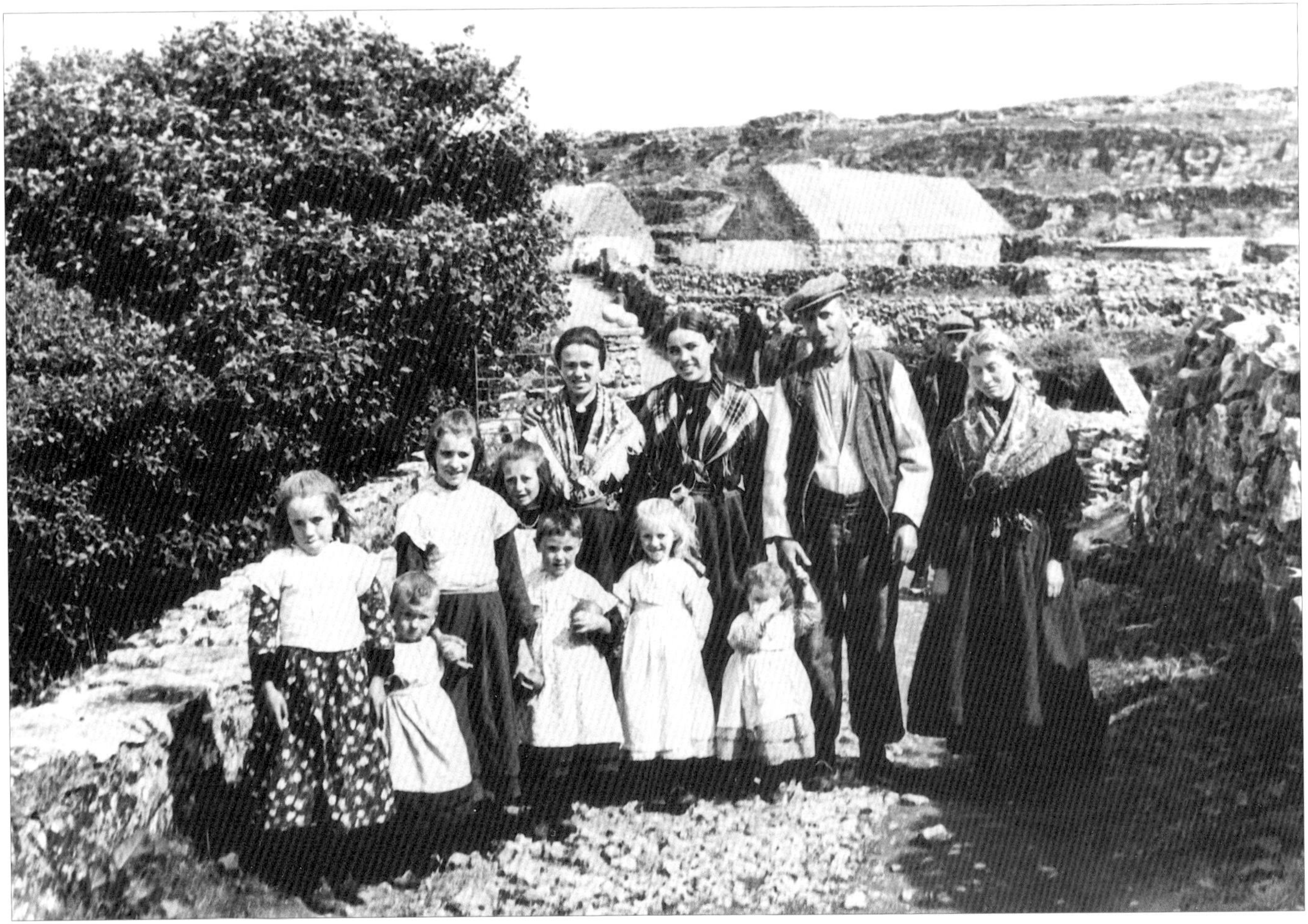

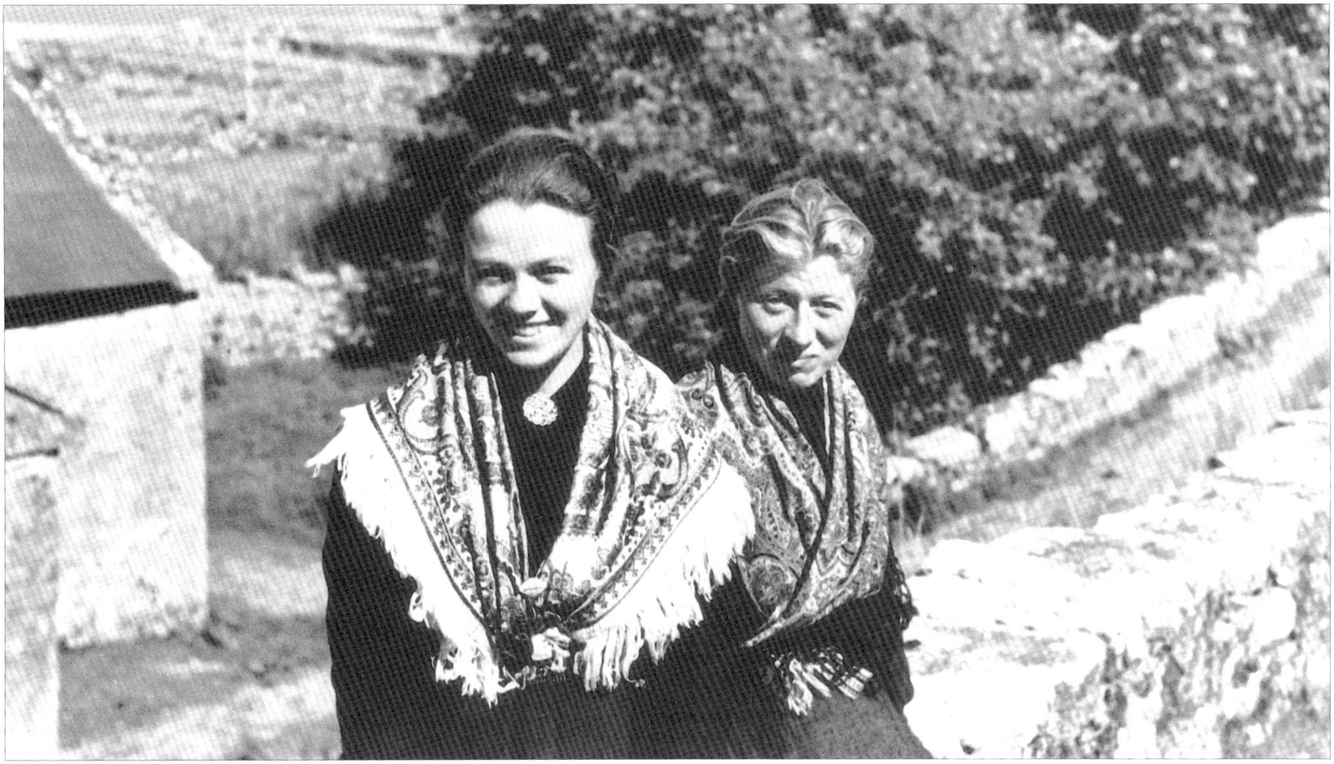

Above: Nora Faherty and Margaret Folan of Inis Meáin. *Below, left to right:* Pádraig Dara O'Conneely and Colm Mór Faherty (Baile an Mothair), Inis Meáin, and Michael Hernon of Kilronan, Inis Mór.

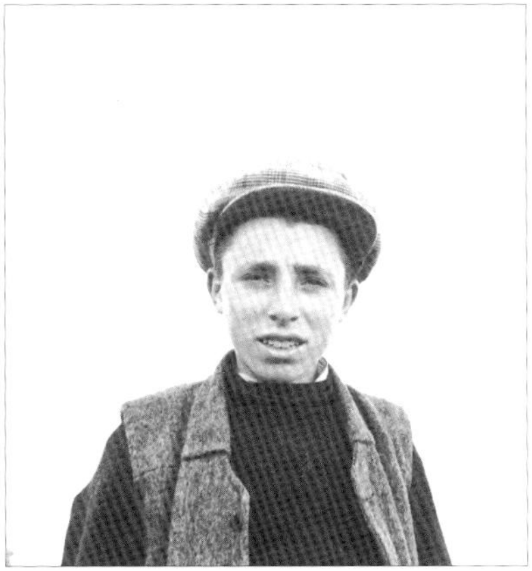

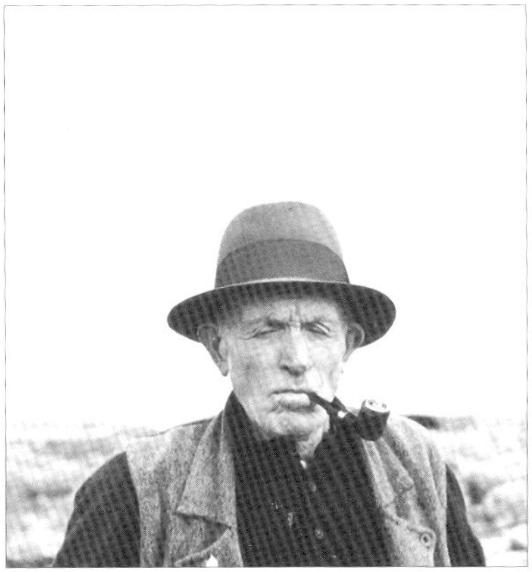

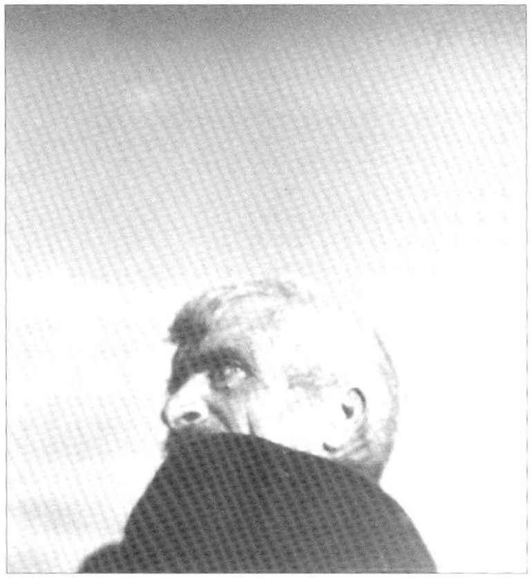

On their way to the wedding. From the left: Mary Kelly, Pauline Conneely, Annie O'Donnell, Bridie O'Donnell and Delia Mullen.

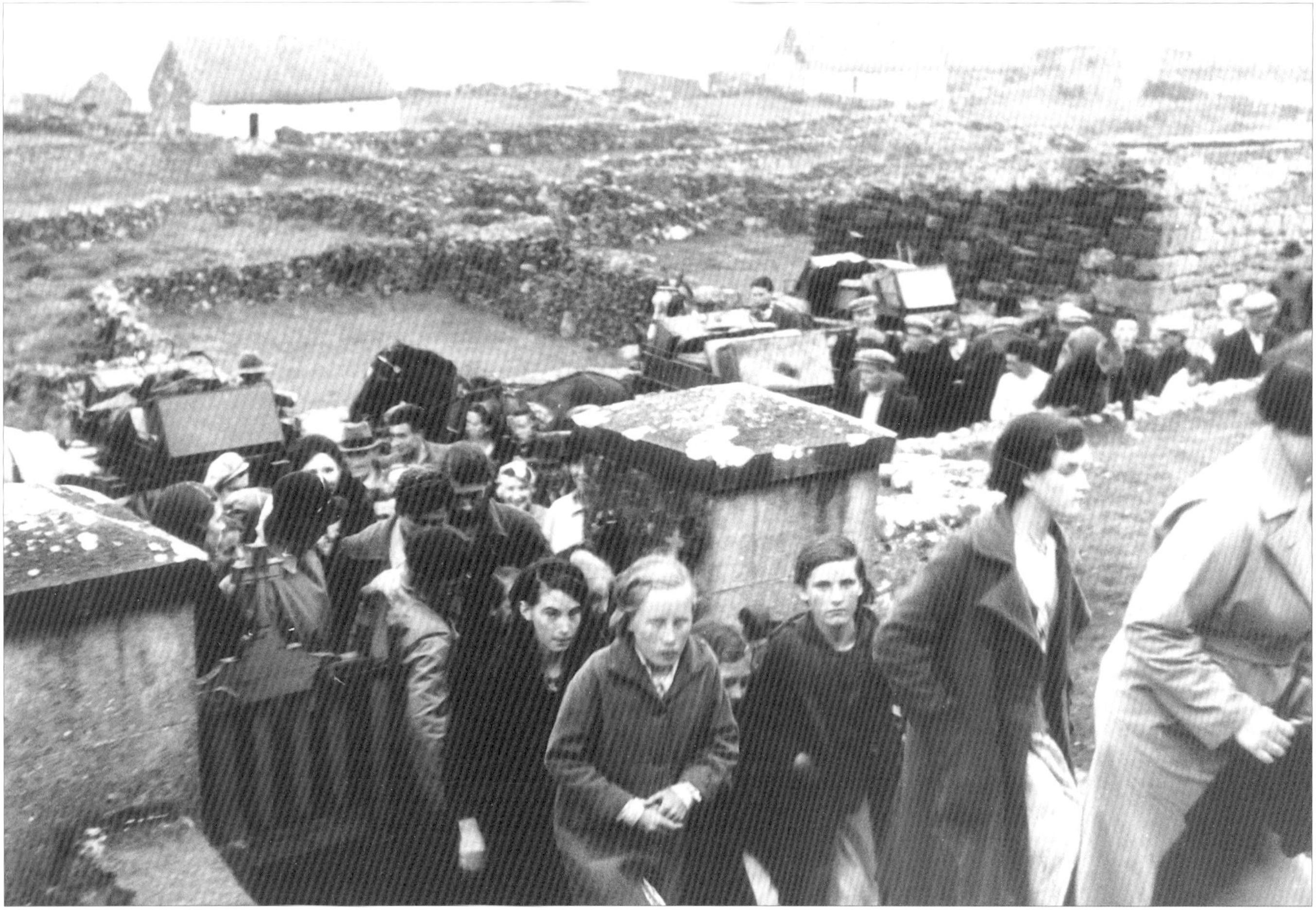

The wedding ceremony at Oughill Church. Today the altar rails have been removed and a red curtain conceals the arches behind the tabernacle. A statue of the Sacred Heart now stands where the doorway leads into the sacristy.

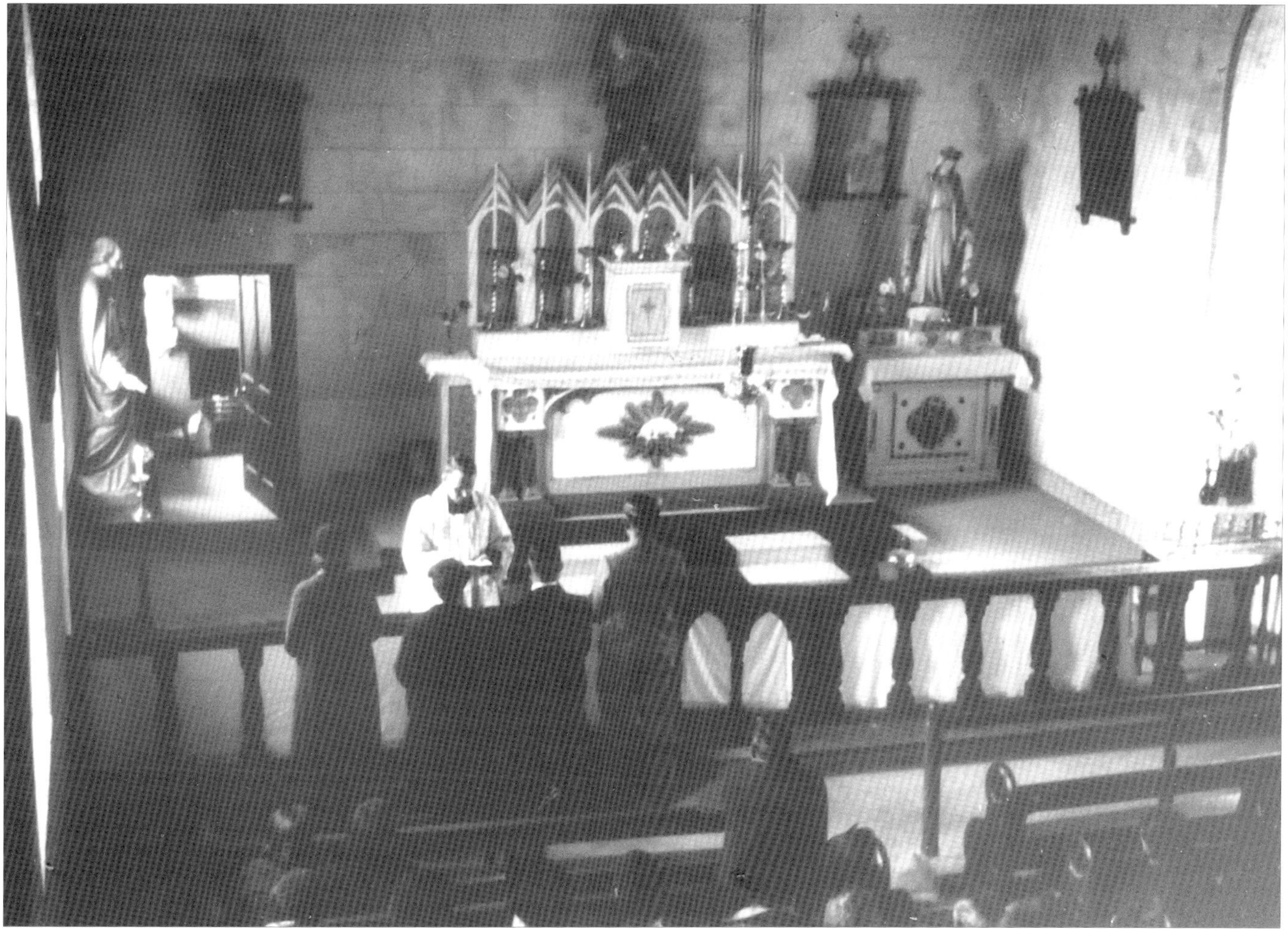

After the Wedding: On the roadway outside Oughill Church are Martin Tom Dirrane (standing) with Bridget and Mary-Ann Kilmartin on his side-car.

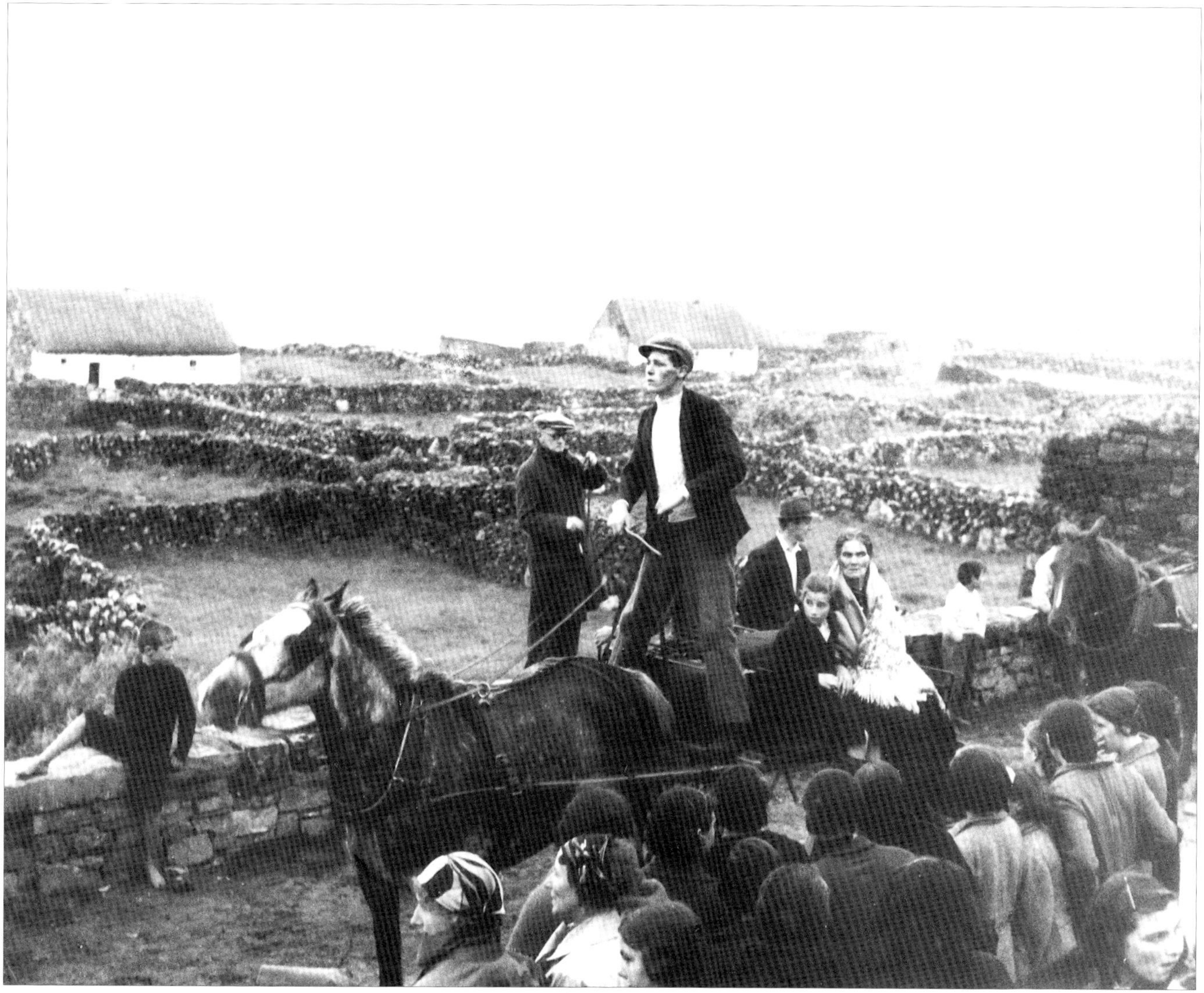

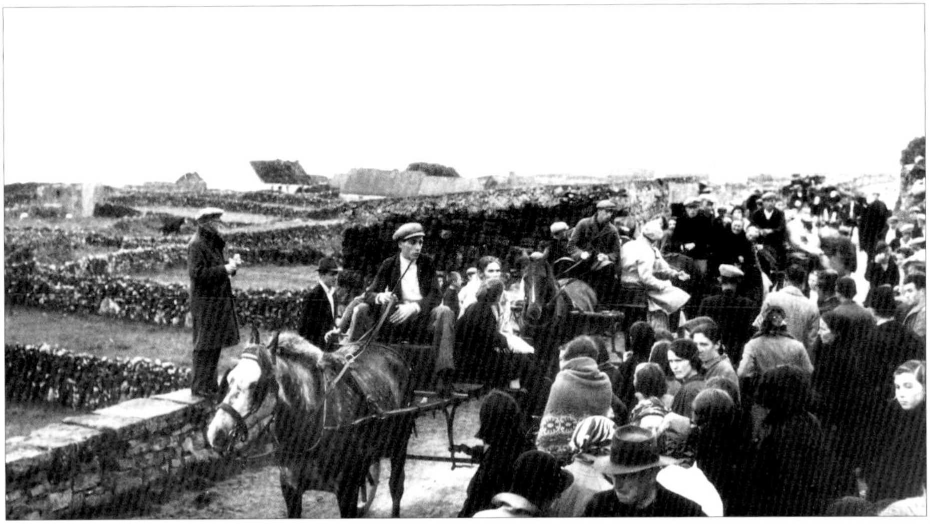

Left: After the Wedding. On the roadway outside Oughill Church are Martin Tom Dirrane driving the leading side-car with Bridget and Mary-Ann Kilmartin as his passengers. Looking on are the O'Donnell girls and the Conneely girls.

Below: After the Wedding. Patín Flaherty is 'playing the box' and the driver of the side-car is Pat Mullen. He and his white horse featured in Robert Flaherty's film, *Man of Aran.*

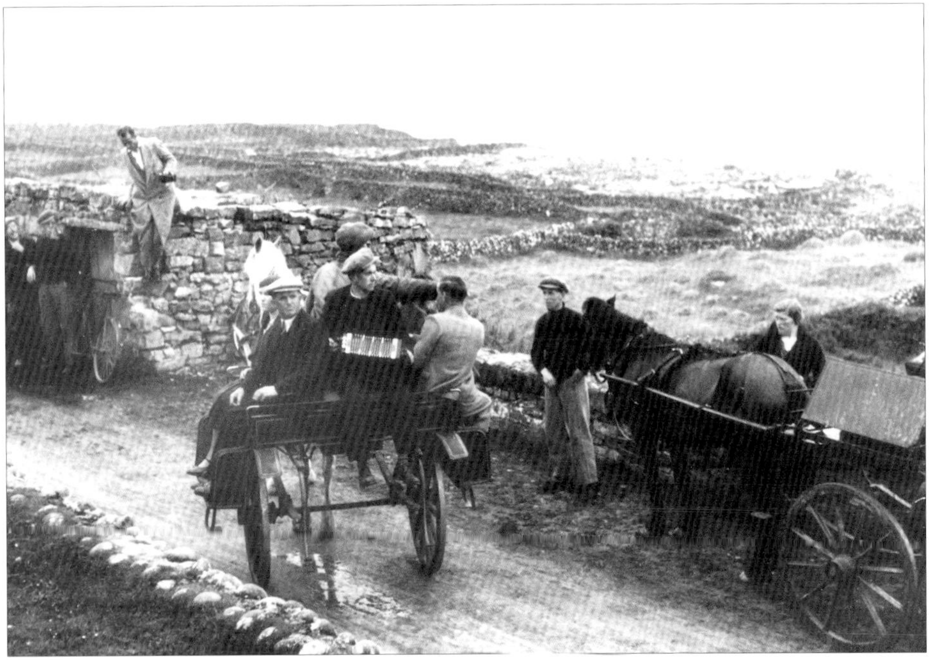

Chapter VIII

The Aran Lifeboat

The first time Father Browne visited Aran, in 1925, there was no lifeboat. The Galway Bay Lifeboat Station, as it is called, opened in 1927 at Kilronan with the crew trained *in situ*. The first lifeboat, named the *William Evans*, had formerly served at Rosslare. It was an open boat with an engine of eighty horsepower.

When Father Browne photographed this lifeboat and its crew in 1938, the coxswain was John Gill, the mechanic was Joseph Doyle, the bowman was Patrick Flaherty and the members of the crew were William Gorham, Patrick Gill, John Flaherty and Tom Flaherty. All seven men were awarded medals for their bravery on the night of 16 August 1938 which was the first time they were called upon to mount a major rescue operation.

On that night the Milford Haven trawler *Nogi* (registered in London) ran aground a little over half a mile from the lighthouse on Straw Island at the north-east end of Inis Mór. In fierce winds and heavy seas two islanders rowed to the rescue in their currach and managed to get a rope on board the stricken trawler. Then the rope broke. One man managed to grab the trawler's anchor and was rescued by its crew. The other was carried away in his small boat.

A sister trawler, the *Hatano,* radioed for help and then launched a boat with four men on board. This boat immediately got into difficulties and was swept towards the rocky coast.

As soon as the SOS message was received at Kilronan, the crew of the *William Evans* was assembled and put to sea. On their way to the *Nogi* they rescued the four men from the *Hatano* and took their boat in tow. When they reached the trawler which was now lying sideways on the rocks, the three Flahertys, along with Patrick Gill and William Gorham, jumped into the boat they were towing and managed to row alongside the *Nogi.* They took six trawlermen on board and rowed them to the safety of the *William Evans*. Then they went back and rescued the remaining five trawlermen in the same way.

Next, the search began for the Aranman who had been carried away in his currach. Eight hours later he was found, suffering from exposure and exhaustion. He was taken on board the *William Evans* and lived to tell the tale.

By this time the wind had abated and the seas had become calm. The four trawlermen from the *Hatano* were able to return to their vessel in their own boat. The lifeboat then returned to Kilronan after fifteen hours at sea. Father Browne was on hand with his camera to record their arrival.

A final interesting fact about the Aran lifeboat. Although not in the charter of the R.N.L.I. which operates the service, the Aran boat used to act as a marine ambulance up to the arrival of the air service. Injured people and expectant mothers were ferried to the mainland as an act of mercy and there handed over to land-based ambulances.

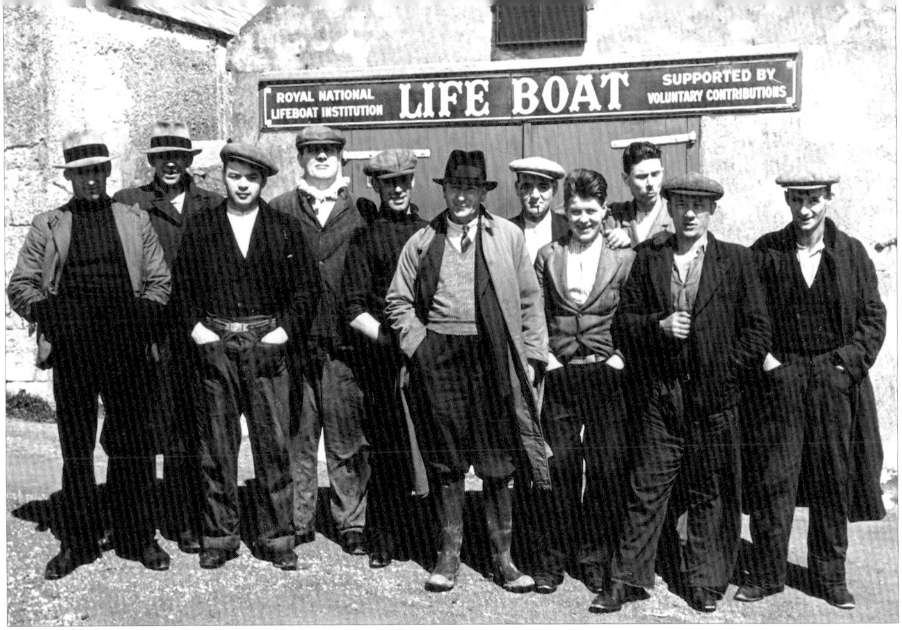

Left: The crew of the Aran lifeboat with survivors from the trawler *Nogi.*

Below: The R.N.L.B. *William Evans* returning to Kilronan after fifteen hours at sea. On board with the crew are three Welshmen who were rescued from the trawler, *Nogi.*

Right: Another day on the *William Evans* as it returns to Kilronan. On board from the left are Joseph Doyle, John Flaherty, John Gill and Patrick Flaherty.

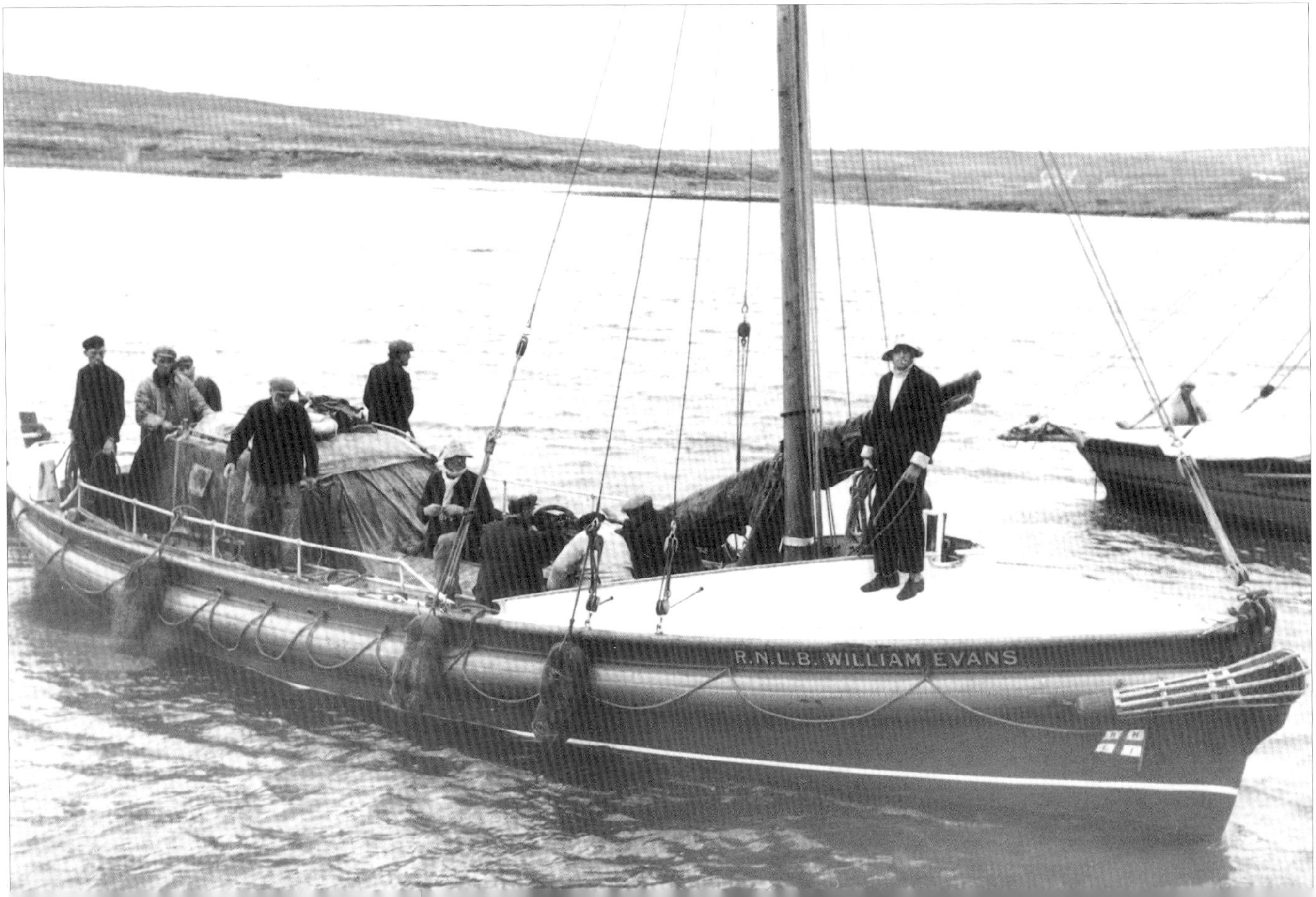

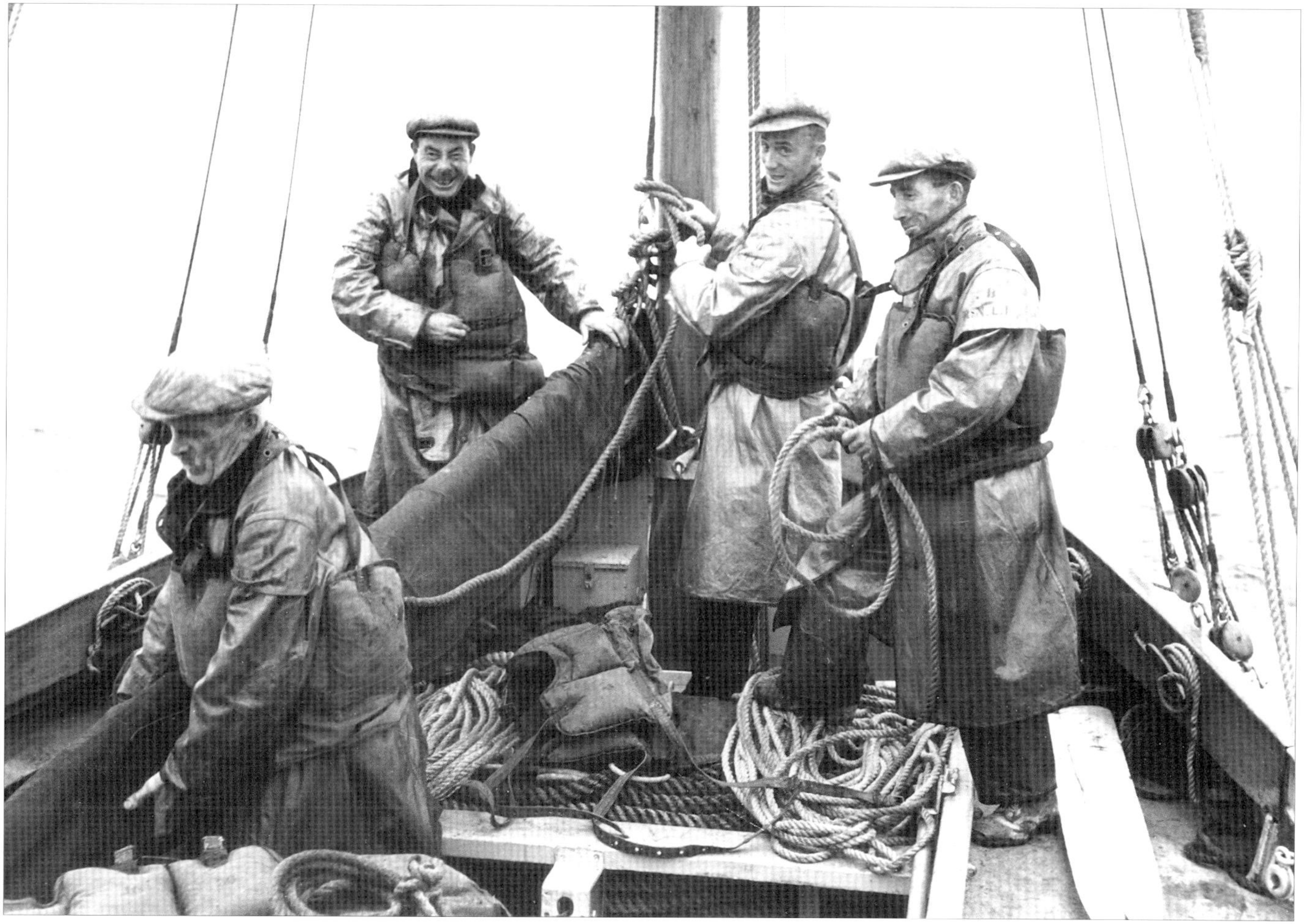

Lifeboatmen with their gear. In front, from the left: John Gill, Patrick Flaherty and John Flaherty.

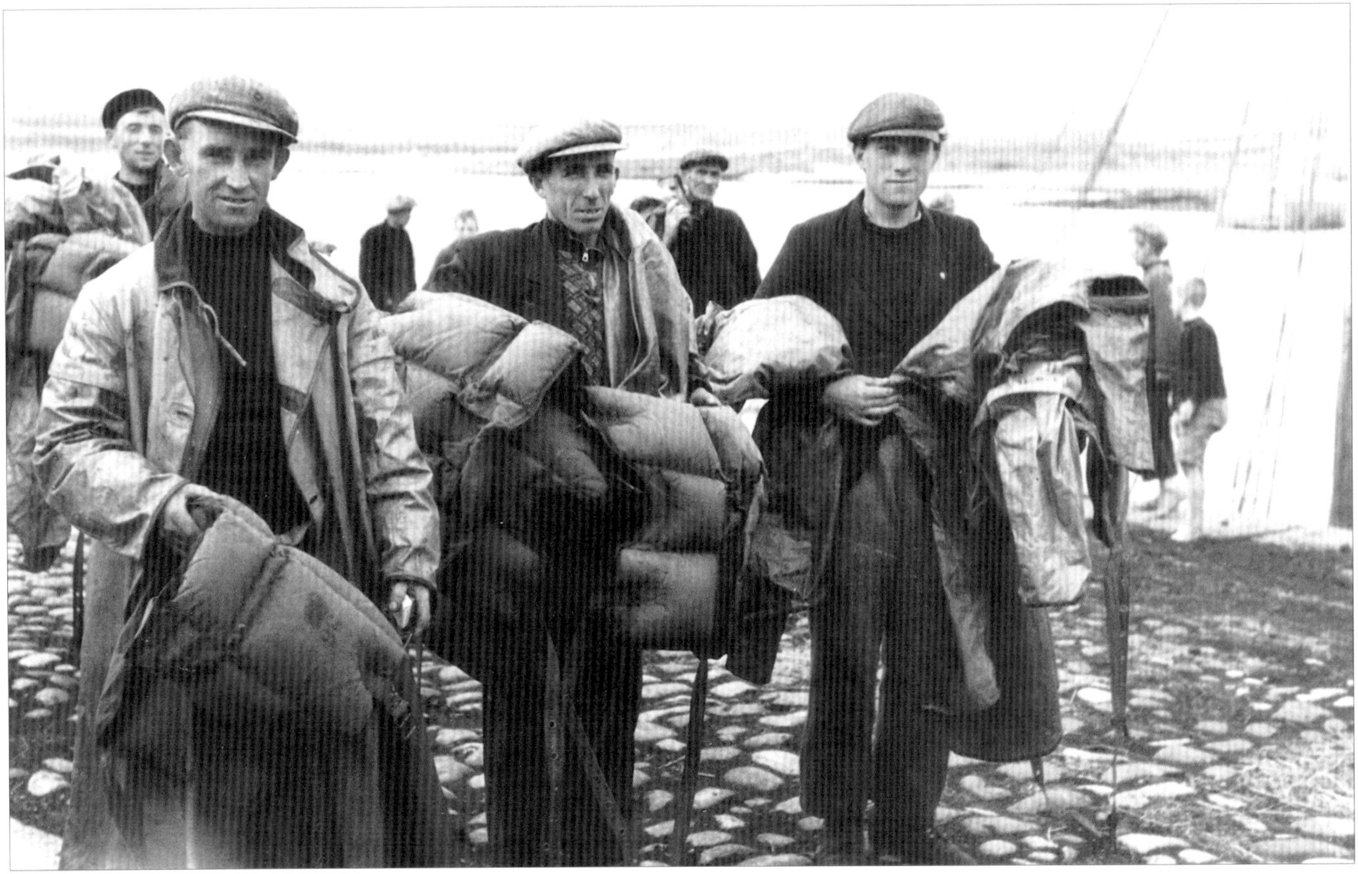

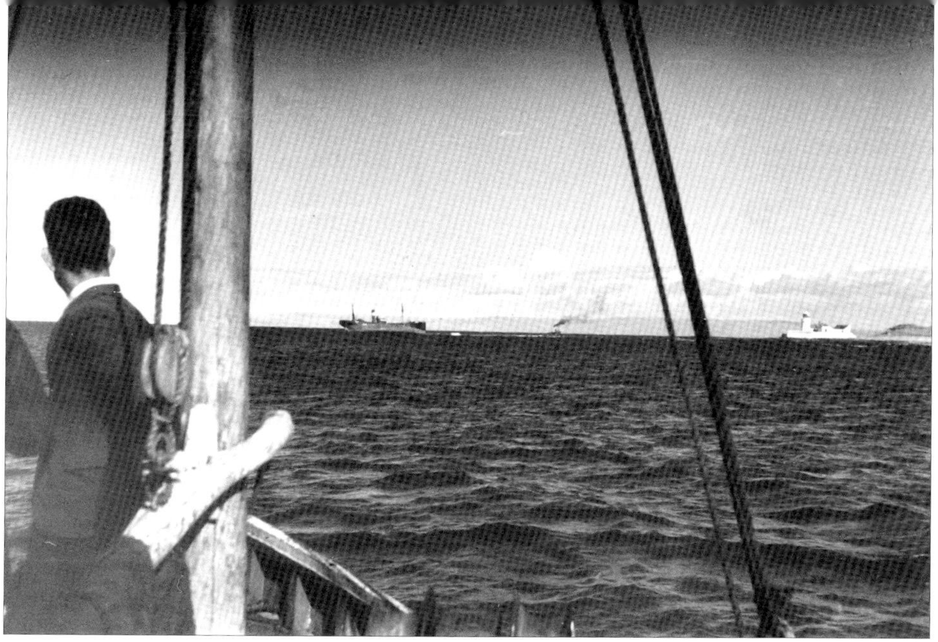

The wreck of the Welsh trawler, *Nogi*, which went aground on Straw Island on 16 August, 1938. The lighthouse on the right was constructed in 1857 and manned until recently. It is now automatic.

Below: This close-up of the *Nogi* was taken by Father Browne from the deck of the *Dun Aengus* when he was leaving Aran at the end of August, 1938.

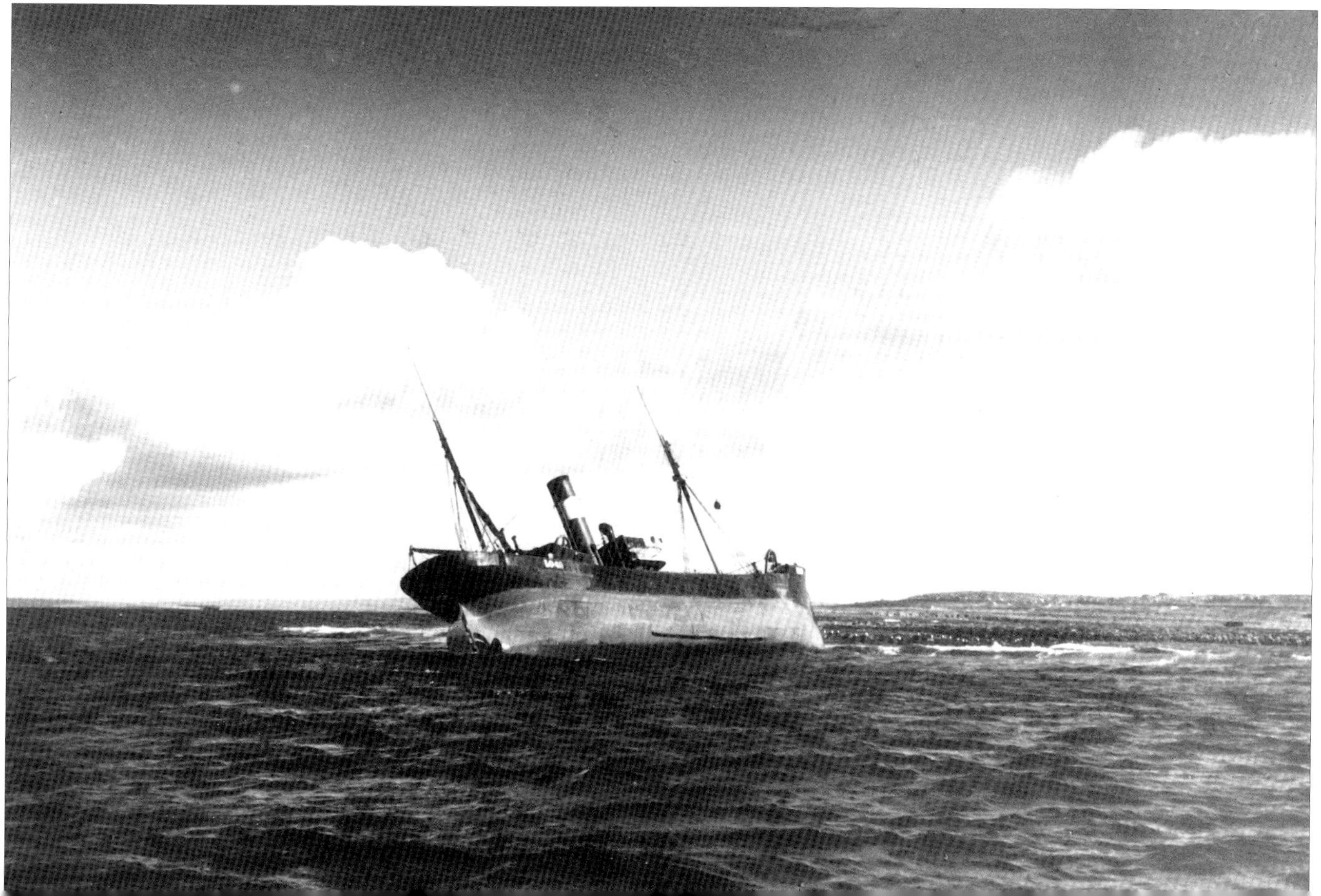

Farewell to Aran. Father Browne's final photograph taken on board the *Dun Aengus* at the end of August, 1938, as he was leaving Kilronan for Galway.

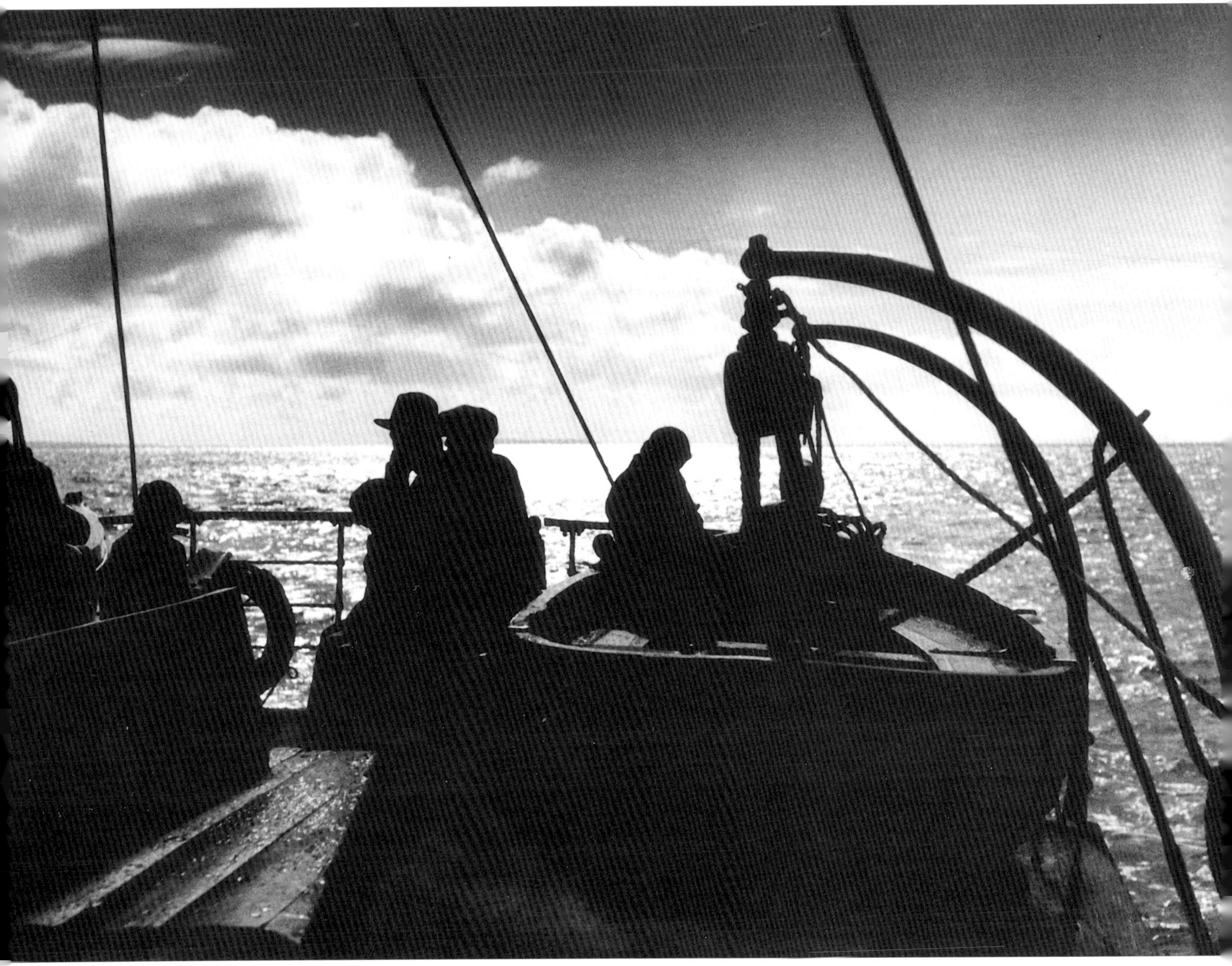